THE

FAT

LADY

AND THE

KINGDOM

D1512106

GEORGE R. KNIGHT

THE
FAT
LADY
AND THE
KINGDOM

**Adventist mission confronts
the challenges of institutionalism
and secularization.**

GEORGE R. KNIGHT

Pacific Press Publishing Association
Boise, Idaho
Oshawa, Ontario, Canada

Edited by Jerry D. Thomas
Designed by Dennis Ferree
Cover art by Mary Rumford
Typeset in 11/13 Janson Text

Library of Congress Cataloging-in-Publication Data:

Knight, George R.
  The fat lady and the kingdom : Adventist mission confronts the
challenges of institutionalism and secularization / George R. Knight.
      p.   cm.
  Includes bibliographical references and index.
  ISBN 0-8163-1259-1
  1. Seventh-day Adventists—Membership. 2. Adventists—
Membership. 3. Mission of the church. 4. Seventh-day Adventists—
Missions. 5. Adventists—Missions. 6. Sabbatarians—Missions.
7. Sabbatarians—Missions. I. Title.
BX6154.K565 1995
286.7'32—dc20
                                                                95-3388
                                                                   CIP

95 96 97 98 99 • 5 4 3 2 1

Contents

A Word to the Reader

Mission is what the Seventh-day Adventist Church is all about. Mission is the only reason for the denomination's existence. Yet Adventism in the 1990s is in danger (especially in such places as North America, Western Europe, and Australia) of settling down as merely another nice comfortable denomination (or social club).

The problem? Jesus hasn't come! Beyond that, some Adventists have begun to wonder if He ever will. Continuing time has spawned the fruits of secularization, disorientation, and institutionalism in the church. The extension of time has mothered every problem currently faced by Seventh-day Adventists. And yet time goes on and on and on.

How is the church to relate to its dilemma of history that will not stop? How can it maintain its identity in a world faced by wave after mega-wave of change?

Those questions are among the most serious ever faced by the denomination. They undergird every chapter of this book.

I have been deeply concerned for the past few years about Adventism's identity and where Adventism is going. That concern has resulted in several articles, book chapters, and papers that focus on Adventist mission and the problems of secularization, change, and institutionalism that threaten that mission. Those articles, chapters, and papers are brought together in this book in order to put them in more permanent form and, more importantly, to call the church to face its challenges, mission, and possibilities openly, honestly, and (hopefully) courageously.

The time has come in the church for forthright talk about the questions raised in these chapters and the challenges faced by the church. Adventism is at a crossroads similar to that faced by the denomination in the 1890s as it moved toward massive restructuring in the early part of the twentieth century. That restructuring did not come without risk and pain, but eventually it did take place. The result was a new lease on life and reinvigorated mission to the world. Similar reassessment and courageous, eyes-open action is needed as the denomination prepares to enter the twenty-first century.

The Fat Lady and the Kingdom addresses many of the problems faced by the church and puts forth certain suggestions toward a remedy. On the other hand, the book does not systematically develop a full-blown set of remedies. The reason is partly because no one knows the full remedy and partly because significant discussions of remedies can only take place after the questions, threats, and possibilities have been thoroughly discussed and explored by all sectors of the church in dialogue.

The issues raised in this volume are not merely the business of administrators and academics. They are of concern to the church as a whole. This book is a call to Christian responsibility for that discussion and, beyond that, to the utter necessity of honesty and courage as we Adventists face the shape, identity, and mission of our church in the future.

The chapters that follow are generally scholarly, but not calmly so. Most of them have been written with more than a bit of passion and anguish. I love my church and long to see it as healthy and whole as possible during its remaining time on planet Earth.

I firmly believe that the key to that health is closely tied to Adventism's faithfulness to its end-time mission as portrayed in Revelation 12 and 14. When Adventism loses its understanding of itself as an end-time people with a prophetic message, it will have become *merely* another denomination largely (or almost exclusively) concerned with shepherding those sheep already in the fold and *merely* with social action. Those things are good in themselves but they are only a part of what Adventism as the personification of the third angel of Revelation 14 is all about.

It is my prayer that this book will be a blessing to those who read it and to my church, and that it will stimulate both healthy vision and movement toward readjustments where needed. Remember as you read that the key word in each of the chapters is *mission*. Mission is Adventism's reason for being.

I would like to express my appreciation to the various periodicals and publishing houses listed under "acknowledgements" below for permission to reprint each of these chapters. I have done only minimal editing on most of the chapters. The bulk of that editing has had to do with updating and the removal of redundancies. However, in a few cases I let some redundancy stand where it was demanded by the flow of argument in a chapter.

I should also note that I have more fully treated the centrality of mission to Adventist development in *Anticipating the Advent: A Brief History of Seventh-day Adventists* (Pacific Press, 1993). That volume is the only history of Adventism written from a missiological perspective. It presents the larger context for many of the topics treated in the present volume.

I would also like to express my appreciation to Bonnie Beres for typing this manuscript, to Russell Holt of Pacific Press and Werner Vyhmeister of the Seventh-day Adventist Theological Seminary for encouraging its publication, and to the administration of Andrews University for providing financial support and time for research and writing.

I trust that this volume will be a blessing to its readers as they grapple with some of Seventh-day Adventism's most important challenges as the church prepares to enter the twenty-first century.

George R. Knight
Berrien Springs, Michigan

Acknowledgments

Each chapter in this book has been previously published or has been delivered as a formal paper. In nearly every case the wording and content remain essentially the same except for minor editing. The foremost exception to that statement is chapter 5, the second half of which has been nearly totally rewritten due to the need for updating and meeting the needs of a vastly different audience. The other chapters have seen some editing of content to lessen obvious redundancies.

Prior publication and/or presentation of each chapter is as follows:

"The Fat Lady and the Kingdom" was published in the *Adventist Review* on February 14, 1991.

"The Life Cycle of a Chuch" was published as "Adventism, Institutionalism, and the Challenge of Secularization" in *Ministry* in June 1991 and formed a major component of "The Hardening of Ecclesiastical Arteries: The Fate of the Apostolic Church and the Future of Adventism"—a paper presented as part of the G. Arthur Keough Lectureship at Columbia Union College on March 20, 1992.

"Challenging the Continuity of History" was originally delivered as a part of the G. Arthur Keough Lectureship on March 21, 1992. It was later published by *Ministry* in December 1992.

"Church Structure: Help or Hindrance to Mission?" was first published in the *Adventist Professional* (an Australian periodical) in March 1992.

"From Shut Door to Worldwide Mission" was first delivered at the University of Hamburg at a symposium on the history of German Adventism on October 11, 1989. It was later published in B. Ed. Pfeiffer, Lothar Träder, and George R. Knight, eds., *Die Adventisten und Hamburg: Von der Ortsgemeinde zur internationalen Bewegung* (Frankfurt am Main: Peter Lang, 1992).

"Adventism's Missiological Quadrilateral" was first delivered on August 5, 1992, at a symposium on the development of Adventism in eastern Africa at the University of Dar es Salaam and the Mbagala Spiritual Centre in Dar es Salaam, Tanzania. It is also being published in the spring of 1995 as a chapter in a book entitled *Development of the Seventh-day Adventist Church in Eastern Africa* (Dar es Salaam: University of Dar es Salaam Press, 1995).

"Mission and Institutional Vitality" was first published as "Spiritual Revival and Educational Expansion" in the *Adventist Review* of March 29, 1984. That article was later expanded and published as "The Dynamics of Educational Expansion" by the *Journal of Adventist Education* in April-May 1990.

"Mission and Lifestyle" was first published in Bailey Gillespie, ed., *Perspectives on Values* (La Sierra, Calif.: La Sierra University Press, 1993).

"The Mainspring of SDA Mission" is a slightly expanded version of the final chapter of George R. Knight, *Millennial Fever and the End of the World: A Study of Millerite Adventism* (Boise, Idaho: Pacific Press, 1993). In essentially its present form it was published as "Adventism at 150" in *Ministry* in October 1994.

"Occupying Till He Comes" was first presented as a paper to the Adventist Society for Religious Studies in Chicago on November 18, 1994.

I would like to express my appreciation to each of the book publishers in the above list for permission to republish the material in the various chapters and to each of the periodicals and institutions noted above for providing earlier forums for the various articles and papers.

Part I

Warming Up to the Topic

Chapter 1

The Fat Lady and the Kingdom*

"The church is like unto a fat woman returning from a shopping spree" (Matthew 13:4494).

My mind's eye grapples with a woman both obese and sweating profusely—a woman standing before a door with arms full of precious packages.

Our parabolic friend faces a crisis. She is unable to open the door to enter her house to put her bundles down. If she reaches for the door handle, she will drop and ruin some of her packages, but if she continues to cling to her packages she will never pass through the doorway.

Her predicament is a catch-22. That is, no matter what choice she makes, she loses something. The only question is, Which option represents the greater loss?

There she stands: sweating, frustrated, and venturing toward constructive thought from time to time—but not too much thought, lest it cause pain or force her into action. She is torn between two alternating

---

*When I first used this title some years ago, my editors and myself wrestled together over its wording—all of us keenly sensitive to avoid sexist stereotypes. After a multitude of alternatives proved unworkable, we fell back on the title as you see it, finding it most in keeping with the images of Scripture in both Testaments. It is my hope that the book's readers will look past this detail to the chapter's message.

desires: (1) to enter her rest and (2) to keep hold of all her packages. Torn by conflicting motivations, she is unable to act on either. The result is more sweat and indecision as she stands within an arm's reach of her goal.

Interpretation

Like many of the parables in Matthew 13, this one demands an explanation. Fortunately, the symbolism is really quite simple.

The woman may be likened unto the Seventh-day Adventist Church, which in its maturity has grown "rich, and increased with goods," and has "need of nothing" (Revelation 3:17).

The many packages may be likened unto the church's structures and institutions, of which the Adventists have a superabundant supply in at least four different wrappings—educational, ecclesiological, medical, and publishing.

The door may be likened unto the way into the kingdom of heaven, with the door handle being the mechanism of entrance into the kingdom. In other words, the handle symbolizes Adventism's evangelistic mission to the world.

The parable's dynamics are also quite self-evident. The aim of the woman is to enter the kingdom of heaven through the doorway. She stands on the brink of ultimate victory, but, and here is the catch, she has been trapped by her own success.

Through scrimping, saving, and sacrificing she has accumulated a large number of institutions and structures. In fact, she has so many that her chief administrators spend a large and crucial bulk of their time attending board meetings and trying to solve the increasingly insurmountable problems of these institutions in a rapidly shifting complex social system.

These problems, however, do not tempt the woman to lay down the packages, because as time has passed *she has increasingly gained her identity through the size, number, variety, and quality of her packages. She has become addicted to packages and package holding.*

The threats facing her packages have actually had the opposite effect on our lady friend. She chooses to grasp the threatened packages all the more tightly. Ever more of her energy, means, and attention is spent tending the growing number of packages. Thus the sweat! Thus her inability and even unwillingness to let them go and reach for the door handle. The end result is that the packages inhibit her entrance.

There is a cruel paradox in all of this. After all, the sole function of the church's structures and institutions ought to be to facilitate the fulfill-ment of mission. Yet in our lady friend's case, they have just the opposite effect. There is something definitely wrong when the church falls into the role of furthering the mission of semiautonomous institutions rather than those institutions furthering the mission of the church.

As Robert Folkenberg (then president of the Carolina Conference) pointed out in the June 1989 *Ministry*, there is nothing wrong with institutions and structures in themselves, but these entities need to be examined from time to time to make sure they are serving their intended purpose efficiently.[1] After all, with the passage of time there is a kind of dysfunctional gravity that tends to pull organizations down from their original purpose. In other words, *the preservation of the structure and/or institution gradually overtakes mission as the predominant concern.* Robert Michels refers to this phenomenon as the "iron law of oligarchy."[2]

Five Stages

These "degenerative processes" are to be expected in an aging church. Sociologist David Moberg points out that churches, like other organizations, pass through five stages in their life cycle. These stages he labels as: (1) incipient organization, (2) formal organization, (3) maximum efficiency, (4) institutional, and (5) disintegration. It seems that the Seventh-day Adventist Church in North America is teetering on the divide between stages 3 and 4.[3]

In stage 3, leadership has a less emotional emphasis than in stages 1 and 2 and is dominated by statesmen, an increasingly rational organiza-tion replaces charismatic leadership, historians and apologists arise, formal structure develops rapidly, and institutions tend to operate with their intended mission in view. North American Adventism entered stage 3 early in the twentieth century.

In stage 4, the institutional stage, formalism saps the group's vitality, leadership comes to be dominated by an established bureaucracy "more concerned with perpetuating its own interests than with maintaining the distinctives that helped bring the group into existence," administra-tion centers on boards and committees that tend to become self-perpetuating, and institutions tend to become masters rather than servants.

It is Moberg's stage 4 that much of Adventism has definitely entered. Like the early Christian church at 150 years of age, Adventists are following a hallowed historic pattern. The thing to note, however, is that stage 5 is labeled "disintegration."

Is life then hopeless? Is the church merely a helpless cog in a sociological machine? *No!* Not unless it fails to take corrective action. As Moberg points out, the process may be reversed; it is not inevitable.

On the other hand, sociological drift will take its deadly toll unless the church decides *consciously* to take *heroic action.* That is, the fat woman in a gutsy sort of way must choose to reevaluate her philosophy of packages and package-carrying. *She must choose consciously whether to gain her identity from mission or from institutionalism.* Intelligent thought on the topic will be both radical and courageous—radical in the sense of the magnitude of the changes that may need to be made to become functional, and courageous, since these choices must be made in the face of entrenched bureaucracies.

As one looks at our special and much-loved Adventist fat woman, it seems that all her packages have major problems. And those problems are complicated by the fact that all the church's packages (institutions and structures) are tied to each other at their deepest level. This implies that to change one part means to make significant changes in the whole. *Adventism does not need tuning up; it needs radical revolution in the fullest meaning of the word if it is to continue to be truly functional in its mission.* And *mission*, as you know by now, is the key word in this essay. Contribution to functional mission in the most efficient and efficacious manner must be the *only* criterion in the church's reevaluation of its structures and institutions.

Unfortunately, institutions and structures don't like change. Their bureaucrats and professionals are equally guilty in avoiding change, as if it were leprosy or AIDS. *The history of the Adventist Church indicates that it never makes needed structural changes of a major sort until it is on the brink of organizational and financial collapse.* My present point—given the current condition of Adventist conference, education, medical, and publishing structures—is that the time of disaster may not be too far off.

Toward Radical Change

Perhaps what is needed for the successful accomplishment of Adventism's only mission is not more institutions and structures, but fewer. Perhaps the need is not to argue whether we should do away with union conferences or combine local conferences in North America, but to do away with both, creating in their wake some twenty regional administrative units that could serve constituencies that have moved out of the horse-and-buggy era and now have access to modern means of communication and transportation.

Beyond structural changes, perhaps the denomination would be better off if its leaders were spiritual bishops rather than international business executives. Are there no ways of delegating business functions to business people so that our "bishops" can once again become spiritual leaders? Too often, it seems, in the current structure, spiritual leadership gets sidetracked or delegated in the process of attending to the urgent and legal necessities of holding the packages or tending the institutional machine.

Beyond functional shifts toward the accomplishment of mission in conference structure, the North American Division needs to ask (and answer) hard questions concerning its institutions. For example, can the division afford to continue to operate thirteen small collegiate institutions? Or are there alternatives—such as consolidation in patterns that capture the advantages of both bigness and smallness? And would it be helpful if some of our hard-earned educational dollars went to support "live-in, eat-in" Adventist student unions at selected non-Adventist universities that could supply social interaction, an Adventist living atmosphere, and credit-generating classes in "philosophy" to help students learn to integrate and evaluate "secular" knowledge in the light of the Adventist worldview? The church also needs to examine the function of "tribal regionalism" in blocking the efficient operation of Adventist education.

Difficult questions must also be faced in regard to Adventist publishing and medical work in relation to the church's mission. One certainly wonders if the hundreds of millions of dollars and large number of people employed in the health system couldn't be reinvested in ways that are more functional toward spiritual ends.

The publishing work also needs to come into the twentieth century. Certainly the effectiveness of the operation of multimillion-dollar printing presses ought to be questioned. Publishing houses (editorial establishments) would be able to cut production costs drastically through the use of competitive bidding on printing jobs. Beyond that, the entire literature evangelist system needs to be rethought and retooled to meet the challenge and opportunities of a late-twentieth-century market.

To Recapture the Mission

As readers of this chapter might have guessed, I am concerned about my church. I fear that in too many cases the church and its institutions have become a "jobs program" and that institutional survival has become an end in itself. Reevaluation and revolution must put mission back on center stage, if we are to stem the drift toward dysfunctionality.

The self-image of Adventism needs to be refocused on mission rather than on packages. Some of our precious packages will have to be dropped before we can grasp the door handle to the kingdom, while others will need to be rewrapped.

My message, in the metaphor of my opening remarks, must be: *"Wake up, fat lady, before it's too late!"*

---

1. Robert S. Folkenberg, "Church Structure—Servant or Master?" *Ministry*, June 1989, 4-9.
2. Michels is quoted in ibid., 4.
3. David O. Moberg, *The Church as a Social Institution: The Sociology of American Religion*, 2d ed. (Grand Rapids, Mich.: Baker, 1984), 118-125. Moberg's five stages will be more fully treated in chapter 2 of this book.

Part II

The Threat of the Present Versus the Challenge of the Future

Chapter 2

The Life Cycle
of a Church:

Adventism, Institutionalism, and the
Challenge of Secularization

Churches in their second century face problems their founders never had to deal with. Two of those problems are institutionalism and secularization. Churches, like people and other organizations, pass from infancy through adolescence into adulthood and eventually have to face the problems of dysfunction that aging brings.

The early church fell into this pattern, as did the Reformation churches and the Methodist movement. The present chapter will examine the problems and challenges of the Seventh-day Adventist Church as it faces the same issues in its second century. In the process we will survey the life cycle of a church, some of the dilemmas that hinder reform, the "problem" of success, and the possibility of avoiding what appears to be the course of history as churches move from being movements to machines to monuments.

Before beginning our journey, it should be noted that this chapter is based upon sociological analysis. It is important to realize that sociological analysis is only one way of viewing the church. As such, it supplements other viewpoints, including the most important perspective—the biblical/theological. While sociological patterns do not predetermine religious history, it is significant that church after church has followed the same pathway to institutionalism and secularization. The challenge set forth in this chapter is to recognize those patterns as they apply to Adventism so that such knowledge, through God's grace, might be utilized deliberately to "correct" the course of Adventism. Whether Adventism will be successful in this respect remains to be seen. But one of the great lessons of church history is that such a course correction will not be the product of either accident or ignorance.

The Life Cycle of a Church

David O. Moberg describes five stages in the life cycle of a church.[1] His analysis sheds a great deal of light on the development and current status of Adventism, even though his model does not provide a perfect correlation.

Before examining Moberg's stages of development, I would like to suggest some qualifications. First, a church may exhibit the characteristics of several stages at the same time, even though it is predominantly in one or two stages at any given time. Second, different individual members, congregations, or ethnic or national subdivisions of a church may be at different stages at the same time. Third, my comments on Adventism will focus on generalizations regarding the worldwide Seventh-day Adventist Church, with an emphasis on the North American Division.

Stage 1: Incipient Organization

Moberg's first stage is that of "incipient organization." Sects, he claims, usually develop out of unrest and dissatisfaction with existing churches, often being stimulated by the lower classes who complain about the clergy, the "corruption" of privileged groups, or denominational complacency. The unrest may arise out of a crisis that the parent church has failed to meet satisfactorily.

With the rise of leadership, a new cult or sect emerges, often as a reform movement within the parental body. Emerging sects are characterized by "a high degree of collective excitement," "unplanned and uncontrolled emotions" in public situations that "may lead to a sense of bodily possession by the Holy Spirit," and physical reactions. "Charismatic, authoritarian, prophetic" leadership is characteristic of this stage.

The stage of incipient organization is a fairly accurate description of Sabbatarian Adventism between 1844 and 1863. Arising out of the failure of the existing denominations to accept William Miller's premillennial views and the unwillingness of the majority of the post-disappointment Millerite Adventists to embrace the biblical truths of the seventh-day Sabbath and the ministry of Christ in the heavenly sanctuary, the Sabbatarian advent band emerged as a separate "sect" between 1844 and 1850.

By that time, three strong leaders—Joseph Bates, James White, and Ellen G. White—had risen to bind the emerging group together through a series of conferences and a periodical. Their combined leadership may easily be characterized as having charismatic, authoritarian, and prophetic aspects. Formal organization was a taboo for most adherents during this period, with some claiming that the first step toward organizing a church was the first step toward forming another Babylon. Their leadership style would not fit well into the Adventism of the 1990s.

Beyond leadership styles, one doesn't have to read very far in the first volume of *Testimonies for the Church* or other early Sabbatarian Adventist literature to pick up the charismatic flavor of their worship. The work of the Holy Spirit was much in evidence through such manifestations as visions, healings, being slain by the Spirit, and even a few instances of speaking in tongues.[2] In many ways, if not most, the early Sabbatarian Adventists would find themselves distinctly uncomfortable in Adventism as we know it today.

Stage 2: Formal Organization

Moberg describes the second stage as being characterized by formal organizational identity. The group formulates and publicizes its goals to attract new members, who in turn are asked to commit themselves by formally joining the group. The organization develops a creed "to preserve and propagate orthodoxy," and emphasizes the differences between the new sect and non-members. Symbols are developed that reflect the group's theological orientation.

Stage 2 often sees the development of an emphasis on behaviors that deviate from those of the surrounding society. Thus, writes Moberg,

> the use of automobiles, neckties, tobacco, instrumental music, cosmetics, or wedding rings may be considered sinful; card playing, movie attendance, dancing, or military service may be tabooed. Thus codes of behavior are developed and enforced; these distinguish members from others and often draw persecution or ridicule that increases in-group feelings and strength.

In addition, "agitational" leadership forms gradually abate as stage 3 is approached.

The stage of formal organization represents Seventh-day Adventist development between approximately 1863 and 1900. The year 1863 saw the formation of the General Conference of Seventh-day Adventists—an organizational step that had been preceded by the formation of the first local conferences in 1861 and the choice of a name in 1860. Such a move was a giant step away from the free-flowing, "anti-Babylon" stance of many adherents in the previous decade.

Following rapidly on the heels of formal organization came Ellen White's June 6 health reform vision (just 15 days after the formation of the General Conference), which proved to be a mighty step forward in the development of a distinctive Seventh-day Adventist lifestyle package. In addition, the mid-1860s saw the denomination take its position on noncombatancy, take special interest in the issue of personal adornment, and establish its first health-care institution. The early 1870s saw the publication of Adventism's first formal statement of beliefs, the development of its first permanent educational institution, and the sending of its first foreign missionary. Persecution over the breaking of Sunday laws in the 1880s and 1890s and continuing adverse discrimination on the basis of its Millerite heritage helped strengthen the young denomination's in-group feelings.

By 1900 Adventism's lifestyle and doctrinal positions were well established, and the church supported a rapidly expanding system of missions, conferences, schools, hospitals, and publishing houses around the world. Beyond that, leadership was becoming progressively more formal and "administrative," as opposed to being informal and charismatic. By the turn of the century, however, the denomination had outgrown its 1863 organizational structure. Reorganization was crucial if the church was to continue to operate effectively. This brings us to Moberg's stage 3.

Stage 3: Maximum Efficiency

If stage 1 is viewed as toddlerhood and stage 2 as childhood, then stage 3 in the life cycle of a church should be seen in terms of youthful vigor and young adulthood. Moberg labels the third stage as that of maximum efficiency.

During stage 3, statesmen dominate leadership and organization becomes increasingly rational. Formal structure rapidly develops as executives, boards, and committees are added to meet the needs of the growing organization. Official leaders perform their duties "enthusiastically and efficiently"; and rituals and administrative procedures, although regularized, are still viewed as means to the end rather than as ends in themselves. Programs of action tend to be formulated in light of rational consideration of relevant facts. Growth during the period of maximum efficiency is often very rapid.

Stage 3 also sees the rise of historians and apologists for the faith. This period witnesses the group move psychologically from the position of despised sect to one of near-equality with recognized denominations. Hostility toward other groups diminishes and "the fanatical resolution to maintain sharply different ways relaxes." As an illustration Moberg goes out of his way in the first edition of his book (1962) to point out "the gradual acceptance of Seventh-day Adventists into fundamentalist circles [through the aid of Walter Martin and Donald Grey Barnhouse in the late 1950s]."[3]

While Adventism may have been achieving public acceptance by the 1950s, the denomination undoubtedly had entered into Moberg's stage of maximum efficiency in 1901. That year saw the administrative reorganization of the General Conference along a more rational line. It also witnessed the election of Arthur G. Daniells to denominational leadership. Daniells was the first president who could be viewed as a "statesman."

The 1901 General Conference session also witnessed the development of union conferences and the present departmental structure at all levels of the church. The departments replaced semi-autonomous organizations, whose varying programs had been impossible to coordinate. The appointment of the first vice-president of the General Conference took place the next year. Subsequent years and decades saw the development of numerous committees, boards, and other entities to forward the work of the church. The organizational changes begun in 1901 set the stage for unprecedented denominational growth around the world. The early decades of the twentieth century also saw the development of the denomination's historical/apologetic literature under such writers as J. N. Loughborough, M. E. Olsen, A. W. Spalding, and F. D. Nichol.

If a specific date can be given for Adventism's arrival at "adulthood," it may best be seen as 1956, when the denomination had the "right hand of fellowship" extended to it by Donald Grey Barnhouse, editor of *Eternity* and a highly influential fundamentalist leader.[4] The acceptance of that fellowship unfortunately (but predictably) split the Adventist ranks between those who viewed it as a step forward and those who saw it as a "sell-out" to the enemy.

Like it or not, however, the denomination had reached its adulthood. Evidence of that transition can be found in the fact that the late 1950s and early 1960s witnessed the capstone being placed on the church's educational establishment, with the creation of two universities, and the hope of developing Ph.D. programs. The important question now became whether the denomination would use its adulthood responsibly.

Even though it seems rather clear that Adventism arrived at the stage of maximum efficiency around 1901, it is much less clear where the denomination is in the 1990s. That may be partly because we lack enough distance from current events to evaluate the flow of recent history properly. It seems that at the present time the denomination may be largely in stage 3, but teetering on the brink of Moberg's stage 4. Another way of saying what needs to be said is that part of the church may be in stage 3, while other sectors are already in stage 4.[5] This picture should become more evident as we discuss stage 4. What is important at this juncture, however, is not that we determine its position, but that we foresee the general pattern of the future if the denominational aging process is not successfully challenged.

Stage 4: Institutionalism

Moberg presents stage 4 as one of great danger. During this stage formalism drains the group's vitality. Its leadership comes to be "dominated by an established bureaucracy more concerned with perpetuating its own interests than with maintaining the distinctives that helped bring the group into existence." Administration tends to center in committees and boards that often become self-perpetuating. The church becomes a "bureaucracy," with mechanisms of the group's structure largely having become ends in themselves.

For individuals at this stage, doctrinal platforms become "venerated relics from the past" and for most "worshipers" organized worship gradually degenerates into a repetitive ritual. At this stage the institution "has become the master of its members instead of their servant, making many demands upon them, suppressing personalities, and directing energies into serving the 'organization church.' "

Stage 4, claims Moberg, sees conflict with the outside world replaced by complete toleration. Conformity to social norms and mores is typical, "respectability" becomes a central quest, and membership standards are relaxed as the church seeks to bring more socially respectable people into the fold. Feelings of group intimacy decline as the growth in membership brings increased heterogeneity and varying dedication, sentiments, and interests. Membership becomes remote from leadership and increasingly passive. Interests and activities once considered "worldly" become major attractions as the church seeks to become a center of community activity. Sermons, meanwhile, become "topical lectures dealing with social issues, rather than fervent discourses" on sin, salvation, and church doctrine.

As noted above, current Adventism has a love/hate relationship with Moberg's institutional stage. Stage 4 is a great temptation for many Adventist leaders and members and a great fear for many others. These ambivalent feelings are sometimes present in the same person or group of people simultaneously.

There are many indications that the denomination at times enters stage 4. These include: church-owned radio stations with almost exclusively classical/cultural programming (except, of course, for the Sabbath hours); the deliberations at the 1989 General Conference Spring Council that set forth arguments for "community wages" for Adventist hospital administrators based on market premises rather than on dedication or denominational mission; and the fact that the church seems to be maintaining an increasing number of personnel and institutions that no longer appear to contribute to the fulfillment of its *primary* goals in the *most effective* manner. Vested interests and tradition loom larger and larger as the church wiggles its toes increasingly in the sands of stage 4.

One of the great challenges facing contemporary Adventism, as it teeters between stages 3 and 4, is to make a healthy adjustment. The church cannot go back to the "old ways" that were effective in the 1930s and 1950s; but to drift into stage 4 means eventual disaster, as we shall see in our discussion of stage 5. The only viable choice is to critique *radically* (yet rationally) the denomination's structures, procedures, policies, etc., and then to retool for reinvigoration at Moberg's stage of maximum efficiency. Such a procedure will take both guts and creativity. We will return to this challenge at the end of this article.

Stage 5: Disintegration

Stage 5 in Moberg's taxonomy is disintegration. Its chief characteristics are overinstitutionalism, formalism, indifferentism, obsolescence, absolutism, red tape, patronage, and corruption. In addition, the institutional machine's lack of responsiveness to the personal and social needs of members causes loss of their confidence.

During this stage many withdraw into new sects or drift without any formal church membership. Many of those who remain in fellowship with the parent body often ignore it in practice or conform to its teachings only halfheartedly. Meanwhile the denomination continues—supported by a leadership with vested interests and by a membership with emotional attachments.

While contemporary Adventism at certain times and places may penetrate the life cycle senility of stage 5, and while some of the denomination's more radical offshoot movements may perceive the church to exist at that level already, it seems that Adventism has a fair piece to go before it is firmly at stage 5. Of course, the better part of wisdom is renewal and reformation at the borders of stages 3 and 4, before further degeneration takes place.

Dilemmas and Roadblocks on the Road to Reformation

Neither renewal or reformation comes easily, however, since religious organizations exist in part to provide stability. Compounding the difficulty is the fact that evolving tradition and structure are often confused with the pristine values of a movement's founders. Religious organizations typically desire to pass on the experience of the founders, their original doctrine, and the lifestyle they set forth as the ideal; but the outcome is often the passing on of the mere forms of the founders without the vitalizing spirit that gave those forms meaning.

Sociologist Thomas F. O'Dea presents five dilemmas that tend to frustrate the renewal and reformation of religious structures.[6] These dilemmas are active to some degree in every stage of the life cycle of a church—from its vibrant infancy through decrepit senility. Their dynamics help push the church down the path to Moberg's disintegration stage. Two of these dilemmas are especially pertinent to this essay, since they interact with the life cycle of the church.

O'Dea's first dilemma is that of mixed motivation—the "Achilles' heel" of social institutions. A movement typically begins with a circle of disciples gathered around a charismatic leader. In the beginning, both leader and followers are single-minded. They know their goal and do not deviate from it. They are not motivated by any external or internal reward structures, such as prestige or benefits, for the simple reason that these do not exist for the new sect.

Subsequent leaders, however, begin to work for the movement for reasons other than merely fulfilling its primary goal. A professional clergy arises that gives stability to the movement, but with stability come many "perks": security, prestige, respectability, power, influence, and the satisfaction derived from the use of personal talents in teaching and leadership. Moreover, keeping these rewards coming tends to become a part of the motivation of the group.

That dynamic opens the door to men and women seeking leadership positions for reasons of self-interest. O'Dea has identified at least three aspects of the more advanced stages of the problem of mixed motivation that further the secularization of the movement as it experiences institutionalism: (1) the emergence of a careerism that is only formally concerned with the movement's goals; (2) bureaucratic growth that may be more concerned with maintaining and protecting vested interests than with accomplishing the movement's original goals; and (3) official timidity and lethargy in the face of problems and challenges, rather than a vital and progressive spirit that is willing to risk all for the accomplishment of the mission.

So while mixed motivation contributes to the survival of the church organization, it also tends to transform the church's goals and values. And that transformation nearly always moves the church toward secularization.

Mixed motivation is not merely a clergy problem. The dedication and motivation of members born into the movement are nearly always of a different type than those of members who have been converted into it as adults. As H. Richard Niebuhr puts it, children brought up in the church "could not be expected to receive the faith with the ardor their parents had manifested nor to experience in a second birth what had in their case been given them in large part with the first."[7]

There may be a vast difference between membership based upon heritage as opposed to membership stemming from conviction. For the first generation of a movement, membership tends to be based on a conversion experience, but for succeeding generations socialization of the young through the process of education and training often substitutes for the more dramatic conversion experience. For many, church membership may mean comfortable social relationships rather than a radical religious experience.

Every church, as it grows older, faces the dilemma of mixed motivation in both its laity and clergy. Adventism has not escaped that secularizing dynamic.

Let us now turn to the other dilemma O'Dea describes as impacting the secularization process—administrative order: elaboration versus effectiveness. As charismatic leadership is routinized in an aging organization, bureaucratic structure increases, and that brings a number of consequences. One of the most serious of those consequences is that structures that are erected to respond to a particular set of problems or opportunities are not dismantled when the reason for their creation passes. As these structures multiply, the movement's complexity increases. While originally the structures solved real problems, their continued maintenance may greatly hinder the solving of later problems.

Obsolete structures may even cause later problems as needed funds are drained off and spheres of competence and authority begin to overlap between departments or institutions. The problems created are considerably complicated by the parallel existence of mixed motivation. Thus "genuine organizational reform becomes threatening to the status, security, and self-validation of the incumbents of office."[8]

Seventh-day Adventism is currently feeling the combined effects of the administrative elaboration and mixed motivation dilemmas. Nearly everyone seems to agree that radical administrative and institutional reorganization, consolidation, and reform are imperative, but few appear to be willing to put their best judgments into action. The result is that a great deal of money and effort is expended in defending the existence of the status quo when these resources might better be used to develop new structures and methodologies to reach the movement's original goals.

Moberg's institutional life cycle pattern and O'Dea's insights on the roadblocks to reform seem to describe inexorable processes. But as we shall see in our concluding section, they can be reversed if a movement senses its danger and is willing to act rationally and courageously.

Before examining possible cures to the "institutional disease," however, we should look at one more factor in the secularization of Adventism.

The "Problem" of Success

"Wherever riches have increased," John Wesley wrote,

> the essence of religion has decreased in the same proportion. Therefore I do not see how it is possible, in the nature of things, for any revival of true religion to continue long. For religion must necessarily produce both industry and frugality, and these cannot but produce riches. But as riches increase, so will pride . . . and love of the world in all its branches. . . . So, although the form of religion remains, the spirit is swiftly vanishing away.[9]

These words from the founder of Methodism state the paradox faced by all religious groups that inspire their adherents to rigorous ethical standards. In their dedication to God, such people work hard and save.

But their very dedication tends to lead them (or more often their children) to worldly success. That success, in turn, leads to more thought about this world than about the next.

These dynamics operate both in the lives of individual Christians and in corporate denominations. Thus Peter Berger can write that one way to prevent a society from becoming secularized is to keep it "in a condition of economic backwardness." Wesley's solution was that Christians should not only gain all they can and save all they can, but also give all they can, so that the kingdom of heaven would retain the allegiance of their hearts.[10] Neither of these solutions, of course, is apt to be as popular as their alternatives.

Seventh-day Adventism currently faces the secularization problems inherent in its success at both the individual and the corporate levels. Its success threatens its goal orientations. This syndrome is evidenced in Adventism when its "conference office types" proudly view their children's (or grandchildren's) graduation from Loma Linda Medical School (as opposed to ministerial training) as the ultimate mark of family accomplishment. On the corporate level the process is evident when maintaining or adding institutions and structures (including conferences) is confused with progress toward accomplishing the denomination's mission. Thus a recent book on Adventism can claim that "to visit the hospitals of the system today is to see an Adventism that is 'of an undenominational, unsectarian, humanitarian and philanthropic nature.' "[11]

Is There Hope?

Can we stop the drift toward secularization? Is there hope? The answer lies in the honesty with which the church faces the problem. Denial will lead to disaster. Defensiveness is even worse. H. Richard Niebuhr sees the "evil of denominationalism" to be "the temptation of making . . . self-preservation and extension the primary object" of its endeavor. Such an orientation merely makes the rise of sects that aim at getting back to the movement's original goals seem "desirable and necessary."[12]

One hundred years ago the Methodist Church in the United States faced the same drift toward success and secularization that Adventism faces today. To many sincere believers it seemed that the church was losing its goal orientation. As a result, the holiness groups arose to aid the denomination in refocusing on what they saw as Methodism's primary goals. The last thing that the first generation of holiness reformers wanted was separation from Methodism. In order to achieve their purposes, however, they began their own printing presses, educational institutions, and camp meetings, and they eventually acquired their own property. The second generation of holiness leaders, having been reared on semi-sectarian thought, took their movements out of Methodism to establish the various Nazarene and Wesleyan denominations.[13] The "success" of the denomination had called forth the sects.

Today Adventism, at 150 years of age, stands in an analogous position to Methodism at the same age. The next 10 years could quite easily see sectarian schism if the maturing denomination does not take corrective action to stem the problems of institutionalization with their secularizing effects.

Fortunately, something can be done if Adventism has the courage to do it. The church is not caught in the clutches of inexorable history.

In his valuable study of the early Christian church, Derek Tidball hints at the dynamics of reversing the institutionalization/secularization process.[14] Tidball turns to Paul's advice to Timothy and suggests that it arose partly from the apostle's desire to stem the problems inherent in an aging church. Tidball emphasizes three of Paul's admonitions.

First, Timothy was "to guard the original aim, teaching and life of the church" (see 1 Timothy 1:19; 4:16; 6:20; 2 Timothy 1:14). Too often people hold firm to the wrong things. "We must hold firm to principles and revealed truths, not to forms, traditions, and structures which are vehicles that conveniently or aptly express those principles in any one age."[15] The church needs to evaluate constantly and critically its true goals and aims and to bring its structures and programs into line with those goals.

Second, Paul urged his younger colleague never to forget his "battle-torn" circumstances (see 1 Timothy 1:18; 4:16; 6:12; 2 Timothy 2:4). The moment Timothy relaxed vigilance, all sorts of secondary issues would sidetrack him. Churches and their leaders need to maintain conscious alertness to what is happening to them. Only by recognizing the problems and challenges and taking efficient action can any church hope to succeed in its mission.

Third, Paul reminded Timothy that he must constantly renew the spiritual resources available to him and his fellow believers in order to maintain the stamina needed for battle (see 1 Timothy 4:14; 2 Timothy 1:6, 7).

Tidball concludes by asserting that to succeed the church needs "to be alert constantly of the peril of mixed motives, the threat of unwieldy bureaucracy, the lessening of standards and the fossilization of principles."[16] Beyond that, he suggests that the church needs to be open to new leaders that God may wish to use for its reform and renewal.

The early church, of course, failed to learn the lessons that Paul sought to teach Timothy. In its second century it began to suffer the ravages of both institutionalization and secularization. Methodism also failed at that point in its second century. The fate of Adventism in its second century awaits the ongoing process of history. The only thing that can be said with certainty now is that Adventism will be swept down the river by the same sociological forces unless it *deliberately chooses and courageously acts* to reverse the patterns of institutionalization and secularization that are part of the dynamics of an imperfect world.

---

1. David O. Moberg, *The Church as a Social Institution: The Sociology of American Religion*, 2d ed. (Grand Rapids, Mich.: Baker Book House, 1984), 118-125. All unattributed citations dealing with Moberg's stage theory in this chapter are taken from this source.
2. For the gift of tongues in early Adventism, see the letters by Ellen G. White and Hiram Edson in *Present Truth*, December 1849, in *Early SDA Periodicals*, 34-36. Ellen White's autobiographical writings provide ample evidence of other charismatic experiences in early Adventism.
3. David O. Moberg, *The Church as a Social Institution* (Englewood Cliffs, N.J.: Prentice-Hall, 1962), 120, 121.
4. See Donald Grey Barnhouse, Are Seventh-day Adventists Christians?" *Eternity*, September 1956, 6, 7, 43-45; T. E. Unruh, "The Seventh-day Adventist Evangelical Conferences of 1955-1956," *Adventist Heritage* 4 (Winter 1977), 35-46.
5. After this chapter was first published in the June 1991 issue of *Ministry*, several readers wrote to me that I was too optimistic about the denomination's condition. One even presented me with the findings of an empirical study he had conducted in Southern California.
6. Thomas F. O'Dea, *Sociology and the Study of Religion: Theory, Research, Interpretation* (New York: Basic Books, 1970), 240-255; Thomas F. O'Dea and Janet O'Dea Aviad, *The Sociology of Religion*, 2d ed. (Englewood Cliffs, N.J.: Prentice-Hall, 1983), 56-64.
7. H. Richard Niebuhr, *The Kingdom of God in America* (New York: Harper Torchbooks, 1959), 170.
8. O'Dea, *Sociology and the Study of Religion*, 248.
9. John Wesley, quoted in Max Weber, *The Protestant Ethic and the Spirit of Capitalism*, trans. by Talcott Parsons (New York: Charles Scribner's Sons, 1958), 175.
10. Peter L. Berger, *The Sacred Canopy: Elements of a Sociological Theory of Religion* (Garden City, N.Y.: Anchor Books, 1969), 132; John Wesley, *The Works of John Wesley*, 3d ed. Peabody, Mass.: Hendrickson, 1984), 7:9.
11. Malcolm Bull and Keith Lockhart, *Seeking a Sanctuary: Seventh-day Adventism and the American Dream* (San Francisco: Harper & Row, 1989), 226.
12. H. Richard Niebuhr, *The Social Sources of Denominationalism* (New York: New American Library, 1957), 21.
13. See Charles Edwin Jones, *Perfectionist Persuasion: The Holiness Movement and American Methodism, 1867-1936* (Metuchen, N.J.: Scarecrow Press, 1974); Timothy L. Smith, *Called Unto Holiness: The Story of the Nazarenes, the Formative Years* (Kansas City, MO: Nazarene Publishing House, 1962); Melvin Easterday Dieter, *The Holiness Revival of the Nineteenth Century* (Metuchen, N.J.: Scarecrow Press, 1980).
14. Derek Tidball, *The Social Context of the New Testament: A Sociological Analysis* (Grand Rapids, Mich.: Zondervan, 1984), 134-136.
15. Ibid., 135.
16. Ibid., 136.

Chapter 3

Challenging the Continuity of History:

The Failure of Marxism and the Frustrationism of Adventism

What do Marxism and Adventism have in common?

In the words of Paul, I might answer, "Much in every way." While I do not intend to examine the "every way" similarities, we will take a look at two significant relationships that could be included in the "much."

Marxism: An Eschatological Movement

Marxism is an eschatological (end-time) movement that reflects a great deal of Christian content. Marxism began as a movement with a global mission to usher in the millennium through preaching its own version of the "good news." It might be postulated that the reason Marxism hated Christianity is that it was in essence its rival rather than its opposite. It had its own prophets, scriptures, and stringent ethical codes, as well as its own millennial vision of the last events of Planet Earth.

In short, Marxism was in competition with Christianity in the marketplace of human souls and cosmic ideologies. It was fighting for victory for its own version of the "great controversy."

Generations of idealistic young people have been thrilled with the essential Marxist message—that all people should do "all they can to contribute to the general welfare." Thus individuals should put as much into the collective pot as possible, while taking out only what they need. At its best, that dictum is also near the heart of the Christian ethic.

One reason Karl Marx despised Christianity is that he saw it as an inadequate avenue to millennial bliss. Worse! Christianity was a deceptive lie. It promised the truth, but turned out to be a deception. For example, in place of operationalizing Christian values, Western Christianity, Marx indicated, uplifted the survival-of-the-fittest law of the capitalistic jungle and became a tool for the rich and powerful to control the masses. Thus Marx saw that Christianity was too often not the way of salvation, but "the opium of the people"—a way to get the masses to swallow the medicine of oppression. That insight was not only brilliant; it was too often correct. *For Marx, Christianity had become the antichrist.*

Thus Marx and his followers developed their own "true philosophy"—their own true religion, their own avenue to salvation, and their own road to the millennial kingdom. Their beliefs impelled their missionaries throughout the world.

Marxism, therefore, should *not* be viewed as an economic system, but as an eschatological philosophy in which economic socialism was an essential aspect of reality.

Marxist eschatology was built upon the philosophy of Georg Wilhelm Friedrich Hegel. Hegel's philosophy of history allowed for historical progression through the opposition of opposing forces. Thus every idea or thesis would come up against its opposite or antithesis. The result would be a new resolution or synthesis. That new synthesis would in turn become a thesis that would be met by a new antithesis to form a new synthesis, and so on. Thus for Hegel history was progressive and dynamic. It flowed from point A to point B to point C.

But Marx pointed out in his adaptation of Hegelianism that the dialectic would come to an end. The final synthesis would come with the dictatorship of the proletariat, when the egalitarian ideas of socialism at its best would be established forever throughout the world. There would follow a time of peace and plenty for all. The age of the oppressor would be over for all time. The Marxist millennial kingdom would have arrived.

The Flaw in the Marxist Gospel

But the Marxist eschatological dream has obviously failed. Why? What was wrong with its end-time formula?

That is not always an easy question to answer. My own doctoral work is in social reconstructionism (a revolutionary philosophy). Before entering doctoral studies, I had, in my frustration with my church and my personal life, resigned from the ministry and had determined to leave both the church and Christianity, but I needed the answer to life. So I studied social philosophies. Still being a fairly young idealist, I was enthralled with the revolutionary doctrines I was imbibing. In fact, my dissertation was on the theories of George S. Counts, who in the depths of the Depression of the 1930s put fire into the possibilities for educational revolution through his *Dare the School Build a New Social Order?* It was a beautiful theory, built upon the best human values.

But at the end of several years of such study I was forced to ask the hard question: "This is all so beautiful, but why hasn't it worked?"

My answer was that the Marxist and non-Marxist revolutionary spirits of a socialist nature had not taken into account the true nature of humanity and the problem of sin.

It sounds good for rosy-eyed idealists to say that all should put in what they can and take out what they need. But *in practice* people take out as much as possible and put in as little as possible. Thus the fall of Marxist socialism.

But it was built upon good doctrine in part. Many conservative American religionists are going to be shocked when they get to heaven and find out that God is a socialist. After all, He couldn't be a capitalist.[1] The functional strength of capitalism is based upon the insight of the truth of human selfishness—get all you can for yourself at the expense of others. That doctrine is appealing to "normal" people, so capitalism works in a sinful society as long as it is heavily regulated by socialism to keep it from being too brutal. The driving force of capitalism is to maximize profits at the expense of labor. It is a survival-of-the-fittest economic doctrine that arrived at its glory days at the same time as Darwinism and social Darwinism. The strength of capitalism is that it has captured the basic truth on the nature of human selfishness—the centerfold of sin. That is an essential aspect of capitalism's correct vision of doctrinal truth.

However, neither socialism nor capitalism works in a fallen world. Socialism, as Communism found out, needed to be buttressed by capitalistic incentives to get people working, while capitalism, as in the experience of the United States, needed to be softened by socialistic humanitarianism. The real problem for pure socialism as found in idealistic Communism is that while capturing the economic principle of heaven, it missed the driving force that makes things work on earth—it had overlooked human nature and the effects of sin. *It missed the linchpin of the human problem, and thus fell*—and mighty was the fall thereof. *Marxism, in short, failed to take into account the tenacious power of vested interests among both its own leadership and followership.* Thus Marxism failed in its attempt to usher in the millennial kingdom.

Adventism and the Flaw

That brings me to the second major point on the similarities between Marxism and Adventism: the temptation to downplay the force of human nature (the core of sin) and vested interests. (Note: I did not say ignore, but downplay.)

At this point I should say a word about Adventism's vision of itself as a prophetic end-time remnant force in world history. Like Marxism, Adventism finds its roots and purpose in millennial hope; in bringing about the end of human history and the ushering in of the kingdom of God—the final solution, the final dialectical synthesis. Also like the Marxists, such a goal has pushed Seventh-day Adventist missionaries to the ends of the earth.

There is a major difference in the eschatologies, however, since the Marxist solution is basically humanistic. In Marxism the kingdom will be ushered in by human effort. Adventism, of course, with its view of the Bible, cannot take that viewpoint on the end of history. The Adventist solution is not humanistic but theistic: it is God's effort, not humanity's, that will result in the ushering in of the kingdom.

But at this point Adventism's theology often becomes somewhat blurred. After all, is not God dependent upon the remnant church's preaching of the three angels' messages, including the everlasting gospel, "to every nation and tribe and tongue and people" (Revelation 14:6)? And isn't the last great accomplishment of the end-time church the preaching of "this gospel of the kingdom . . . throughout the whole world, as a testimony to all nations; and then the end will come" (Matthew 24:14)? Haven't Adventists believed that the Lord's coming awaits the faithfulness of His last-day remnant people on earth?

In summary, have not we as Adventists to some extent made God's theistic solution dependent upon a humanistic accomplishment? And if so, may we not possibly be tending toward the fallacy that undermined Marxist millennialism?

Now, I am not saying that Seventh-day Adventist theology is wrong or that we should stop our missionary activity, but I am suggesting that we ought to reexamine Adventism's past and present and its possible futures.

That brings us back to the secularizing stages of the church that I described in chapter 2. In that chapter I indicated that churches, like people, go through an aging process and that religious revivals eventually succumb to the process of secularization. Thus repeatedly across history we find that once vital and reforming movements degenerated into denominations that are often preoccupied with maintaining their own existence and traditions. That chapter also pointed out that there are several sociological forces arrayed against the continuity of vital reformation that make it almost impossible for a religious movement to maintain its original intensity and single mindedness toward mission.

Adventism at 150 seems to be moving in lockstep with other religious movements from the early church to the Reformation to Wesleyanism. Each went through a secularizing process that put it off its missiological course by its 150th birthday. It is of crucial importance to realize that *not one major religious revival in the history of Christianity has successfully escaped that process.* None has broken the process of history. None has, in Marxist terms, ended the dialectic.

And why? The answer seems to lie, as I suggested in chapter 2 in discussing the Adventist drift toward secularism and institutionalism, in the dynamics of human nature, including the problems of mixed motivation and vested interests of both individuals and national segments of the church. Those problems not only derailed Marxism and earlier Christian movements, but they could conceivably sidetrack Adventism. At least I see no empirical reason to believe otherwise, given a church that has over-institutionalized, overbureaucratized, and seems to be in the process of becoming increasingly happier with the kingdom of this world.

A lack of insight into the tenacity of human nature in the face of human inability in cosmic affairs eventually ended the Marxist dream. Is it not a *possibility* that the same forces might eventually take their toll on Adventism? To put it another way, are Adventists *guaranteed* a victory in just the way they have always taught it?

Probably not. *It was one of the great fallacies of the first-century Jews to believe that the God of heaven was somehow dependent upon them.* They had carefully read the Old Testament and *correctly* concluded that the *main* line of Messianic prophecy taught that Christ was to come as a mighty king after the order of the conquering David; that an earthly millennium would be set up and that all the faithful from around the world would come to Jerusalem to pay homage to Yahweh; that the Messiah would conquer all Israel's enemies.

The point to remember is that the first-century Jews had come to correct prophetic conclusions. From Isaiah to Malachi the theme of a victorious Israel and an earthly millennium dominate the prophetic literature. On that basis, it is little wonder that the Jews rejected Jesus, who claimed to be the Christ. It must be admitted that Jesus was a Christ who was truly out of harmony with the main prophetic thrust of the Old Testament scriptures. I would suggest that most of us, had we lived in the time of Christ, would have drawn the same conclusions, along with the arrogant one that God was dependent upon the literal Jewish remnant.

The first-century Jews forgot two things: (1) human nature and (2) the right of God to be God in spite of human failure.

They forgot that the prophetic promises fell within the *covenant relationship*; a relationship that promised blessings *if and only if* God's people remained selflessly faithful to Him. The Jews had forgotten the big *"if"* of the covenant: *"If* you obey the voice of the Lord your God, being careful to do all his commandments which I command you this day, [then] the Lord your God will set you high above all the nations of the earth" (Deuteronomy 28:1). "But *if* you will not obey the voice of the Lord your God . . . , *then* all these curses shall come upon you" (verse 15).

God had done all He could for His remnant, but they did not respond in heartfelt allegiance to Him. Human nature overcame them, and they forgot that God could still be God independent of them. Many Jews of the New Testament era had come to believe that God was dependent upon them for the coming of His Messianic kingdom. "If Israel were to keep two Sabbaths according to the laws thereof," cried some of their rabbis, "they would be redeemed immediately."[2] "If," cried others, "Israel repented in one day, the Son of David would come immediately. If Israel would keep one sabbath correctly, the Son of David would come immediately."[3]

"But," Jesus remonstrated with them, "you have missed the boat. You have missed the meaning of the covenantal relationship. Therefore, God can raise up children of Abraham from the stones if need be" (Matthew 3:9, paraphrased). That God is not dependent upon human beings was Christ's message. *God could still be God. He could still act independently to achieve His goals.*

Because of the failure of the Jewish remnant, God altered His eschatological promises and put into action Messianic plan number two. That plan was tucked away in such passages as Isaiah 53 and Psalm 22, passages that were not even perceived as being Messianic. Messianic plan number two was not one of Jewish victory, but of a suffering and rejected servant;[4] a Messiah most Jews could not even recognize because of their fixation on their victory and on God's dependence on them and their actions. Thus, even though the first-century Jews taught a biblically correct end-time doctrine, the first coming of Jesus overtook those students of prophecy as a thief in the night. They were passed over, and God raised up the Christian church to complete the Jewish mission to the world.

The Conditional Nature of Covenant

But once again, it must be noted, the Christian church is also a covenant people. God's New Testament people are still in an *if/then* relationship with the promises of God. They, as God's people, still have to wrestle with the frailty and self-centeredness of human nature. *They still must recognize the fact that God can still be God and independently act to bring the affairs of earth to a close in His own way if His church loses its missiological integrity.*

I would like to suggest that we as Adventists ought to keep our eyes open to the possibility that God might have a plan number two to bring about the end of the Christian age, just as He had for Christ's first coming. We need to keep open the possibility that even in our time the covenant-keeping God has not made Himself dependent upon human faithfulness. Prophetic confidence resides in the absolute certainty of Christ's first and second advents, rather than in any secondary promises concerning those advents or any specific human means of bringing them about.

That distinct possibility first came to my mind in the mid-1960s while reading *Selected Messages*. There we read about the Adventist work spreading "like fire in the stubble." The passage goes on to state that "God will employ agencies whose origin man will be unable to discern; *angels will do a work which men might have had the blessing of accomplishing, had they not neglected to answer the claims of God.*"[5] We generally call attention only to the first part of that passage, while neglecting the if/then language and the plan number two type talk of its second part. Again, Ellen White wrote: "None of us can do without the blessing of God, but God can do His work without the aid of man *if* He so choose."[6]

"There is a deplorable lack of spirituality among our people," Ellen White wrote in the late 1880s. She had seen that "self-glorification was becoming common among Seventh-day Adventists and that unless the pride of man should be abased and Christ exalted we should, as a people, be in no better condition to receive Christ at His second advent than were the Jewish people to receive Him at His first advent."[7] In another passage she suggests that the great crisis could steal upon Seventh-day Adventists as a thief,[8] and in yet another place she claims that if a church is not faithful to God it can be bypassed in His work, *"whatever" its "position."*[9] She also drew a lesson from history: "Because," we read of the ancient Jews, "they failed of fulfilling God's purpose, the children of Israel were set aside, and God's call was extended to other peoples. If these too prove unfaithful, will they not in like manner be rejected?"[10]

From the perspective of Ellen White, God did not grant the Adventist Church any immunities.

> In the balances of the sanctuary the Seventh-day Adventist Church is to be weighed. She will be judged by the privileges and advantages that she has had. If her spiritual experience does not correspond to the advantages that Christ, at infinite cost, has bestowed on her, if the blessings conferred have not qualified her to do the work entrusted to her, on her will be pronounced the sentence: "Found wanting." By the light bestowed, the opportunities given, will she be judged.[11]

Again, in the midst of the Minneapolis crisis Ellen White deplored the fact that Seventh-day Adventists had been acting like other churches. She went on to say that "we hoped that there would not be the necessity for another coming out."[12] Thus Ellen White at the very least hinted at the possibility of Adventist failure. Finally, in 1883 she wrote that "it should be remembered that the promises and threatenings of God are alike conditional."[13]

After coming across a few such hints of alternative eschatological futures in the writings of Ellen White, I began to read the Bible for hints of a backup eschatological vision in the New Testament, that, like plan number two in the Old Testament, *might possibly read clearer or even differently by way of hindsight.*[14]

The first text that came to my mind was Luke 17:26-30:

> As it was in the days of Noah, so will it be in the days of the Son of man. They ate, they drank, they married, they were given in marriage, until the day when Noah entered the ark, and the flood came and destroyed them all. Likewise as it was in the days of Lot—they ate, they drank, they bought, they sold, they

planted, they built, but on the day when Lot went out from Sodom fire and sulphur rained from heaven and destroyed them all—so will it be on the day when the Son of man is revealed.

Now, there are two ways to read that eschatological passage. The first understands it from God's perspective, as reflected in Genesis 6:5. Speaking of the time of Noah, Genesis claims, "the Lord saw that the wickedness of man was great in the earth, and that every imagination of the thoughts of his heart was only evil continually." From that viewpoint, the eating and drinking and marrying became degenerate signs of the times.

But there is another perspective in Luke 17: the human interpretation of what was happening in the days of Noah and Lot. Their contemporaries were eating, drinking, marrying, buying, selling, planting, and building until the very day of their destruction. In other words, life appeared to be going on just like normal. "So will it be on the day when the Son of man is revealed." Thus it seems that we should at least admit the possibility that that day could come as a thief to modern-day students of prophecy if the *if/then* covenant obligations have been disrupted.

Jesus told us to be ready, "for the Son of man is coming at an hour you do not expect" (Matthew 24:44). That hour is today and tomorrow. It is a time for which Adventists could be unprepared if they have not even considered the possibility of an eschatological plan number two.

Lessons for Adventism

Now, what can we conclude from all this? *Not*, I would suggest, that the end will definitely come about in a different way than Adventists have always taught. *But* it does seem necessary to conclude that Adventists must allow for the *possibility* (1) that God can close the events of history in a different way than promised *if* the faith conditions of the covenant are not fulfilled by His people; (2) that God still reserves the right to be God; and (3) that He is no more dependent upon modern spiritual "Jews" than He was upon ancient literal Jews.

Furthermore, another possible conclusion is that if Adventism hopes to complete its historic mission it will have to come to grips with the sociological forces of history that eventually spelled failure for Marxism and drove other Christian bodies off their missiological course by the end of their first 150 years. The human factor expressing itself in such realities as secular drift, vested interests that hinder top-to-bottom *radical reform* in Adventist organizational and institutional structures,

and mixed motivation among both laity and clergy can only be overcome by conscious, heroic, and continuous efforts at reform and
revitalization. And those efforts can come only through renewed and
daily surrender in faith to the cosmic God of the covenant.

Adventism needs to come to its individual and collective senses if it
is to maintain meaningful existence.

And, you may ask, "what if Adventism fails to come to a sense of its
contingent/conditional/finite status?" *Then God will still be God, just as
human nature will still be human nature.* He is not short on power or
dedication to bring about the coming eschaton.

----

1. At this point it is important to recognize that the terms "socialism" and "capitalism" are used in
this chapter as abstract economic principles developed by philosophers of the marketplace. As
such, the basic meanings of capitalism and socialism should not be confused with any past or
present expressions of those philosophies in real life.

Too many people have blurred the distinction between American practices and the ultimate
ideals of the kingdom of God. Those in that position might also be surprised to discover that God
is neither an American (or Western European) nor the ruler of a democracy.

The ultimate principles of heaven must not be confounded with the economic and political
necessities of a sinful earth in which no one person or group can be trusted (an insight that led the
ex-Puritan founding fathers to place the system of checks and balances in the United States Con-
stitution) and in which sin pushes individuals and nations in the direction of distorted self-interest. One gets the impression that service and sharing will be of much more concern to the citizens
of heaven than acquisitiveness or the maximization of self-interest.

2. Babylonian Talmud, Shabbath 118b.
3. Jerusalem Talmud, Taanith 64.
4. The presence of alternative eschatologies in the Old Testament should not lead us to discount
the need for the substitutionary sacrifice of Christ under either model. After all, substitutionary
sacrifice is central to the Old Testament, being first hinted at in Genesis 3 and 4 and later high-
lighted by the sanctuary service. On the other hand, the Bible does not explain how the sacrifice of
Christ would have taken place under the victorious-Israel model. The necessity is clear but not
the means. I have treated the centrality of substitutionary sacrifice to the entire Bible in *My Gripe
With God: A Study in Divine Justice and the Problem of the Cross* (Washington, D.C.: Review and
Herald, 1990), 44-60.
5. Ellen G. White, *Selected Messages* (Washington, D.C.: Review and Herald, 1958, 1980), 1:118.
(Italics supplied.)
6. Ellen G. White, *Testimonies for the Church* (Mountain View, Calif.: Pacific Press, 1948), 5:736.
(Italics supplied.)
7. Ibid., 5:727, 728.
8. E. G. White, *Selected Messages*, 3:414.
9. Ellen G. White, *The Upward Look* (Washington, D.C.: Review and Herald, 1982), 131. (Italics
supplied.)
10. Ellen G. White, *Christ's Object Lessons* (Washington, D.C.: Review and Herald, 1941), 304.
(See also 303.)
11. E. G. White, *Testimonies*, 8:247.
12. Ellen G. White, Manuscript 30, 1889, in *The Ellen G. White 1888 Materials* (Washington,
D.C.: Ellen G. White Estate, 1987), 1:356, 357.
13. E. G. White, *Selected Messages*, 1:67.
14. The possibilities of New Testament plan number two in the following discussion are merely
hinted at rather than developed to any extent in this chapter.

Chapter 4

Church
Structure:

Help or Hindrance
to Mission?*

Trevor Lloyd: Welcome back to Australia. You've come at a time when there is more and more concern in many circles over the influence our present organizational structure is having on the mission of the church. Are there many organizations worldwide with comparable approaches to government and administration?

George Knight: Without a doubt, the Seventh-day Adventist church structure has a corporate and bureaucratic flavor about it that is shared by many organizations. However, as far as churches are concerned, it is fairly unique. Like the Roman Catholic Church, Adventism has developed a worldwide hierarchical model. However, Adventism's structure is probably tighter and more unified than that of Catholicism.

Lloyd: What were the early background influences that prompted

---

*This chapter reports a January 1992 interview between myself and Dr. Trevor Lloyd, the editor of the *Adventist Professional* (an independent but denominationally supportive periodical published in Australia). I have wrestled mightily with whether to rewrite this chapter so that it would match the others in format, delete it, or let it serve as an appendix.

I have chosen not to delete the chapter or relegate it to an appendix because it contains material crucial to this book. Furthermore, I have opted to leave it in its original interview format because it says what needs to be said in a forceful and straightforward manner that gets right to the heart of the issues. To rewrite it in more formal style would remove much of its punch and would necessitate a much more ponderous and lengthier chapter.

Adventism toward a particular style of organization?

Knight: At the very outset of the setting up of this church, there were two contrary influences. James White and Joseph Bates came out of the Christian Connection, which regarded organization as a move toward "Babylon"; while Ellen White came of Methodist stock, which saw organization as an effective way to resist the evil one.[1] Fairly early on, in 1861-1863, a measure of organization was adopted as a means of holding property, paying salaries, and providing general direction to the work. There were about 3,500 members in the church at that time.[2]

Lloyd: How influential was the church's missionary expansion of the 1870-1890s on organizational structure?

Knight: Greatly so. By the 1890s, Seventh-day Adventists had entered all the continents and the Pacific, taking with them their publishing work, school program, medical branch, and conference organization. How could this far-flung family in many nations be kept on course? Only by a functional organizational structure that could facilitate its mission. Interestingly, the innovations experimented with in some of the distant regions became patterns for the worldwide church to follow. For example, South Africa taught us departmental organization, and Australasia first introduced the union conference under the leadership of W. C. White and Arthur Daniells.[3]

Lloyd: What were the influences at work at the time of the radical reorganization of 1901?

Knight: Several. For example, communications being as slow as they were at the turn of the century, with decision-making authority centralized at headquarters in Battle Creek, Michigan, the church was threatened with organizational collapse. In addition, the church was feeling the effects of a depression in the mid- and late 1890s more serious in some respects than that of the 1930s. In the midst of this, the innovations from South Africa (church departments) and Australasia (union conferences) were being offered as more efficient ways to organize on the one hand.

While, on the other hand, Alonzo T. Jones and his supporters were harking back to the Christian Connection, Pentecostal/Holiness model where every believer was to be ruled and directed by the Holy Spirit only.[4]

In the face of stagnation due to delayed decision making, of financial crisis, and of Ellen White's promptings for change, the present worldwide, multitiered structure emerged in 1901-1903. It proved to be quite workable for the 78,000-member church of the time and has continued largely unchanged to the present, except for the dividing of the General Conference into divisions.

Lloyd: Ninety years down the track, how is the four-tier organizational system standing up?

Knight: Not all that well. It has not remained flexible enough to keep up with developments both within and without the church. As a result, we now have a bureaucratic structure which appears to be limiting our achievement of mission in some serious ways. Administrators breed administrators and even in times of financial crisis it is hard to decrease their numbers.[5] In spite of the fact that we are in an age of vastly improved transport and communication, in many parts of the world there appears to be more salaried ordained talent behind desks than in frontline pastoral and evangelistic posts.

Lloyd: How are our institutions faring as we look for effectiveness in mission for cost involved?

Knight: It is hardly overstating the case to say that many of our institutions are in a state of crisis. Just as Adventist hospitals around the world witness their costs burgeoning, their mission is being more and more limited. While our earlier sanitariums accepted patients for several weeks and impressed upon them the Adventist lifestyle and message, presently the great majority of hospital patients have short-term visits of 2 to 3 days or less. Thus Adventist health care facilities tend to have minimal impact on the lives of their patrons.

At the same time, our publishing houses and book work are having to support a crippling bureaucratic structure and terribly expensive printing equipment. The upshot is that the overhead has to be added to the price, when a trimmed down publishing bureaucracy and competitive bidding for printing could both lower costs and provide profits for experimentation in new publishing ventures. It is unfortunate that Adventists have seemingly never been able to distinguish between a publishing house and a printing establishment. In addition, the educational arm of Adventism must make renewed efforts at achieving its mission. It needs to demonstrate that its schools are, indeed, making a difference with regard to turning out loyal, committed Seventh-day Adventist Christians.

In short, the denomination's institutional structures need to be totally reevaluated in the light of current realities and new possibilities.

Lloyd: Are there any pointers to what may be promising ways through our organizational crisis?

Knight: We are coming back to the twin problems of 1901—structural inefficiency and crippling cost. These could not be ignored even by an entrenched bureaucracy of the day, and under God's leading a way was found through. Clearly, we have a repetition of the twin crises of the turn of the century.

Lloyd: Is anything being done within the bureaucracy itself to correct the situation?

Knight: A start was made at the Perth Annual Council, in late 1991. However, attention was confined to the top tier of the organization, with the vast bureaucratic structure beneath the General Conference left without attention.

Lloyd: To what extent should we regard the present church organizational structure as divinely inspired and intended to last for all time?

Knight: This question was addressed by Barry Oliver (presently on the staff at Avondale College) in a Ph.D. dissertation completed at Andrews University.[6] His study of the 1901-1903 reorganization makes it clear that the structure set up in Ellen G. White's day cannot rightly be seen as necessarily applying for all time. The basis of the reorganization was functionality for mission. We have the task of facing, under God's leading, the new demands of a new day.

Lloyd: How urgent is the task? Is time running out on us?

Knight: Extremely urgent, but also complex. Presently we have nearly 7,000,000 members in 1992 [over 8,000,000 in 1994], with numbers escalating in third-world countries while barely holding their own in many industrialized nations. By the year 2000, we could have as many believers in Africa as we had in the whole world in 1990. If the church is to be able to manage its worldwide work by the turn of the new century, it should be changing its power base, structures, and administrative style now.

Lloyd: Can you envisage a radically different system of church government?

Knight: Yes, but if we are going to internationalize the government of the church, we must be prepared for solutions as radical as the problem is serious.

The worldwide church is rather like a group of struggling believers in a small locality with a wealthy doctor whose tithe and offerings more than equal the total contributions of the remainder of the membership. In practical terms, how much say should he have? In the Seventh-day Adventist Church, who should be in control—the industrialized world with the finance, or the third world with the membership (something like 85%)? Maybe we could (or should) end up with a bicameral system—as in the United States and Australia—with the "lower" house constituted according to population and the "upper" house according to region.

The problem of reorganization is complicated by the fact that not all parts of the world have the same political sophistication and background in democratic procedures. As the years go by, the tackling of the problem can only become more difficult. A tune-up will not suffice. We need something even more radical than 1901 if Adventism is to successfully meet the challenges of a complex situation.

Lloyd: What is holding us back from making change in the system from top to bottom?

Knight: We are struggling against the inertia of vested interests, and that makes for an uphill battle all the way.[7] Already, as I've said, in many places we have more pastoral talent in the bureaucracy than we have in the frontline. And it must be remembered, once you get above the local conference level, it is largely the bureaucrats who continue, quinquennium after quinquennium, to vote the bureaucrats in.

Lloyd: Would you like to see the status of the local pastor/ evangelist raised?

Knight: In this respect, as in a number of others, we have followed the corporate model of hierarchy and not the biblical model of talents or gifts. We must learn to put the highest salary and the highest status where the real action is—with the local pastor in the local church. And this will require a reversal of the present system of financial and prestige rewards.[8]

At present, the pastor is in the stressful position of receiving pressure from administrators above and from the congregations below. He is supposed to push the church's programs onto the people and get as much as possible from them. More administrators need to see themselves as servants and facilitators rather than as "bosses" or "career bureaucrats." We need to destroy the mentality that treats a move from the pastorate to administration as a "promotion."

Lloyd: What is the alternative to radical change in Seventh-day Adventist church structure?

Knight: We could see the gradual strangulation of the church in the industrialized world. As frustration with the bureaucracy increases, dissident groups will drain away more and more tithe. Amongst those who maintain their loyalty, the more intelligent will be more and more troubled over supporting a system that is not functioning as efficiently as it should.

Lloyd: In conclusion, what brief plea would you like to pass on to persons in each of the groups—administrators, pastors, and laity—as we seek wisdom to plan and courage to carry out radical structural change within Seventh-day Adventist church organization?

Knight: To the church at large: that it realize that the 1861-1863 and 1901-1903 organizational structures were not divinely inspired, but were established to facilitate mission.

To administrators: to not only recognize the need for radical change, but to facilitate the implementation of that change. In addition, to more often emphasize the fact that frontline leadership is of crucial importance, since if the victory does not take place at the front line it will not take place anywhere, in spite of the quality of behind-the-scenes leadership. I would plead for more administrators to recognize the need for more of their "tribe" to utilize their talents and skills in the form of frontline role models for younger and/or "less promotable" workers. There is too much talent allotted to greasing the wheels and watching the baggage. In fact, there are too many wheels and too much baggage.

To pastors: to realize the promise of their position in terms of building up the body of Christ. Too many pastors have their eye on hierarchical advancement rather than on the joy of loving people and developing into first-rate biblical preachers who feed an ever-growing flock. Let the businessmen run the finances of the church and let the deacons "deak." The pastor's job can be the best job and the most important in the church, but it is at present the most underdeveloped. Good preaching, loving pastoring, and convincing evangelization are the greatest needs of Adventism today.

To the laity: encourage and reward responsible reorganization and functional pastoring whenever possible. Make your voice and influence felt for the health of the church. After all, you are the church as much as pastors and administrators. The church is not that "nebulous other"— it is you. Act for your own health. You can make a difference.

---

1. A history of Methodism that emphasizes this point is Charles W. Ferguson, *Organizing to Beat the Devil: Methodists and the Making of America* (Garden City, N.Y.: Doubleday, 1971).

2. The best study of the 1861-1863 organizational developments is Andrew G. Mustard, *James White and SDA Organization: Historical Development, 1844-1861* (Berrien Springs, Mich.: Andrews University Press, 1988).

3. The best study of the 1901-1903 reorganization is found in Barry David Oliver, *SDA Organizational Structure: Past, Present, and Future* (Berrien Springs, Mich.: Andrews University Press, 1989). W. C. White's role in the development of union conferences and the reorganization is discussed in Jerry Allen Moon, *W. C. White and Ellen G. White: The Relationship Between the Prophet and Her Son* (Berrien Springs, Mich.: Andrews University Press, 1993).

4. A discussion of A. T. Jones's theory of administration is found in George R. Knight, *From 1888 to Apostasy: The Case of A. T. Jones* (Washington, D.C.: Review and Herald, 1987), 178-193 and passim. For the Holiness/Pentecostal roots of Jones's theory, see such works as Melvin Easterday Dieter, *The Holiness Revival of the Nineteenth Century* (Metuchen, N.J.: Scarecrow Press, 1980), 107, 115, 217, 219, 247, 248, 250, 251, 256, 258, 259, 262, 268, 292; Edith L. Blumhofer, *Restoring the Faith: The Assemblies of God, Pentecostalism, and American Culture* (Urbana, Ill.: University of

Illinois Press, 1993), 14, 29, 71, 77, 81, 99, 115, 116, 205, 206.

5. The classic study of this phenomenon is "Parkinson's Law or the Rising Pyramid," in C. Northcote Parkinson, *Parkinson's Law and Other Studies in Administration* (New York: Ballentine Books, 1964), 15-27.

6. Oliver, *SDA Organizational Structure.*

7. See Thomas F. O'Dea, *Sociology and the Study of Religion: Theory, Research, Interpretation* (New York: Basic Books, 1970), 240-255.

8. For more on this topic, see my treatment of "The Myth of Up and Down" in George R. Knight, *Myths in Adventism: An Intrepretive Study of Ellen White, Education, and Related Issues* (Washington, D.C.: Review and Herald, 1985), 89-100. See also George R. Knight, "Reschooling Society: A New Road to Utopia," *Phi Delta Kappan* 40 (Dec. 1978), 289-291.

Part III

The Shape of Adventist Mission

Chapter 5

From Shut Door to Worldwide Mission:

The Historical Development of SDA Mission

Seventh-day Adventists currently support one of the most ambitious mission outreach programs in the history of Christianity. As of January 1994, they were sponsoring work in 209 of the world's 236 nations, preaching and teaching in 713 languages, and publishing literature in 206 languages.[1] They have planted their schools, medical institutions, and publishing houses in all parts of the earth, impelled by the driving force of a belief that holds that the second coming of Christ will not take place until "this gospel of the kingdom shall be preached in all the world for a witness unto all nations" (Matthew 24:14).

The extensiveness of Adventist mission outreach is the product of a prophetic consciousness—a consciousness that permits no division of world mission into areas of denominational responsibility for ecumenical cooperation based on Christ's great commission of Matthew 28:19, 20. While accepting that commission as a mission mandate to Christians in general, Seventh-day Adventists have been *driven* by a more specific mission to preach the message of the three angels of Revelation 14 (the "everlasting gospel" linked with the distinctive Adventist doctrines) "to every nation, and kindred, and tongue, and people" (Revelation 14:6-12).

According to Adventist understanding, the end of earth's history will not come until the voice of the three angels has been heard throughout the earth. That view has undergirded and pushed forward the Adventist drive for world mission. It has left Adventism with no choice but to evangelize in every nation. Seventh-day Adventists do not see themselves as one denomination among many, but as God's remnant end-time people (Revelation 12:17; 14:12).

That line of prophetic interpretation has dominated Adventism for more than a century, but such a burden could not have been predicted by the denomination's founders and earliest members. In fact, one of the most important doctrines in the denomination's earliest theology was that of antimission.

Phase I: The Antimission People (1844-1850)

The earliest phase of Sabbatarian Adventist (the Sabbatarian Adventists organized into the Seventh-day Adventist Church in 1863) mission theory and practice can be accurately described as a "shut door" on mission outreach. That concept was not original with the Sabbatarian group, but had been developed by William Miller and his followers in the early 1840s.

Miller and his fellow believers had preached that Jesus would return about 1843 or 1844. They finally established the exact date of Christ's advent as October 22, 1844.[2] Miller likened his message to the "midnight cry" in the parable of the ten virgins (Matthew 25). That parable claims that when the bridegroom (i.e., Christ) comes the door will be shut, leaving some on the outside. "'The door was shut,'" Miller held in the early 1840s, "implies the closing up of the mediatorial kingdom, and finishing the gospel period."[3]

After Christ did not return on October 22, Miller—still expecting Christ's soon appearance in the clouds of heaven—interpreted the shut door as the close of human probation. In December 1844, he wrote:

> We have done our work in warning sinners, and in trying to awake a formal church. God, in his providence has shut the door; we can only stir one another up to be *patient*; and be diligent to make our calling and election sure. We are now living in the time specified by Malachi iii.18, also Daniel xii.10, and Rev. xxii.10-12. In this passage we cannot help but see, that a little while before Christ should come, there would be a separation between the just and the unjust. . . . Never since the days of the apostles . . . has there been such a division line drawn.[4]

During late 1844 and early 1845 the Millerite movement split into several factions, with Miller and the majority giving up the belief that the door of human probation had been shut on October 22, 1844. That revision followed from their view that they had set the wrong date and that the fulfillment of the 2300-day prophecy of Daniel 8, indicating the exact time of the second advent, was still future. Some Millerites, including those who began to accept the importance of the seventh-day Sabbath in 1845 and 1846, held that October 22 was the correct date for the fulfillment of Daniel's prophecy, and that human probation had indeed closed at that time. Thus the Sabbatarian Adventists came to be known to other Millerite Adventists as "the Sabbath and shut door people"—derogatory terms signifying their doctrinal distinctives.

During the shut-door period of Sabbatarian missiology, it was believed that the evangelistic mission of the movement was restricted to those who had accepted the second advent message of the 1830s and early 1840s. The door of probation had shut for all others. So firmly was the shut-door view held that one of the future organizers of the Seventh-day Adventist Church was "nearly refused the message, the individual presenting it [to him] having doubts of the possibility of his salvation because he was not in 'the '44 move.' "[5]

Ellen G. Harmon (later White) was one who held the shut-door position. In 1874 she wrote: "With my brethren and sisters, after the time passed in forty-four I did believe no more sinners would be converted. But I never had a vision that no more sinners would be converted."[6] She, along with her fellow Sabbatarian Adventists, would begin to change their shut-door theology in 1850 and 1851. Meanwhile, they were busy establishing the doctrinal basis for what was evolving into Seventh-day Adventism. Beyond that, through a series of conferences lasting from 1848 through 1850 the leaders of the Sabbatarian Adventists (Joseph Bates and James and Ellen White) were developing a consensus among a core group of believers on those basic doctrines.

James White viewed the post-1844 period as the "scattering time." The disappointed Millerites had been "grieved, driven and scattered upon the mountains." But by September 1849 he could write that

> the gathering time has come, and the sheep are beginning to hear the cheering voice of the true Shepherd, in the commandments of God, and the testimony of Jesus, as they are being more fully proclaimed. The message will go, the sheep will be gathered into the present truth, and the breach restored. All the

powers of earth and hell combined . . . cannot stop the work of
God. Then let the message fly, for time is short.[7]

Thus the years from 1844 through 1850 were a time during which the
Sabbatarian Adventists built a doctrinal and membership base. The shut
door was a necessary period in the movement's development. The
Adventists could not have had a mission of any magnitude during that
period, since until near its end they had no message to preach. Neither
did the movement have a compelling purpose. In 1861 the Seventh-day
Adventist founders recalled that "our views of the work before us were
then [up through the early 1850s] mostly vague and indefinite."[8]

The shut door missionary doctrine was reinterpreted in the early
1850s, largely as a result of conversions to Sabbatarian Adventism of
individuals who had not been through the Millerite movement of the
early 1840s. In 1850, for example, James White reported the conversion
of a man who "had made no public profession of religion" prior to 1845.
The next year White stated that the door was shut to "those who [had]
heard the 'everlasting gospel' message and [had] rejected it," but that the
door of conversion was still open for three classes: (1) "Erring" ex-
Millerites who had not as yet sided with the Sabbatarians, (2) children
coming to the age of accountability, and (3) hidden souls who had not
bowed unto Baal and would be converted in the future. Thus White
opened the door a bit more to account for known conversions, but he
still held that the present task of the Sabbatarian Adventists was to work
for their ex-Millerite brothers and sisters.[9]

In spite of White's rather cautious evaluation of the movement's
mission, within six months he was reporting more converts from the
third category. Then in May 1852 he told the readers of the *Review and
Herald* that "this work is not confined to those only who have had an
experience in the past advent movement. A large portion of those who
are sharing the blessings attending the present truth were not connected
with the advent cause in 1844." Their minds had not been called to it
and, consequently, they had not rejected it.[10] These increasing acces-
sions were forcing a reinterpretation of the shut door.

As early as February 1852 James White had begun to teach explicitly
the open door theory of mission, writing:

> This OPEN DOOR we teach, and invite those who have an
> ear to hear, to come to it and find salvation through Jesus Christ.
> There is an exceeding glory in the view that Jesus has OPENED

THE DOOR into the holiest of all . . . and now stands before the Ark containing the ten commandments. . . . If it be said that we are of the OPEN DOOR and seventh day Sabbath theory, we shall not object; for this is our faith.[11]

The open door missiology had been set forth in principle by Ellen White in November 1848 when she urged her husband " 'to print a little paper.' " It would be " 'small at first,' " but would eventually develop into " 'streams of light that went clear round the world.' "[12] In July 1850 she wrote that those "who had not heard the Advent doctrine [of the 1840s] and rejected it would embrace the truth and take their places" with the Sabbatarian Adventists. Recalling that statement at a later date, she noted that "our brethren could not understand this with our faith in the immediate appearing of Christ." [13]

By the early 1850s the Sabbatarian Adventists not only had a growing concept of open-door missiology, but they also had a theological rationale that would progressively stimulate them to give their distinctive message to an ever-widening group of potential converts. That theological rationale was the third angel's message of Revelation 14:9-12, which contrasted those who eventually would have the mark of the beast with those who kept God's commandments.

As early as 1847 Joseph Bates identified the preaching of the Sabbath as essential to the third angel's message, and by early 1850 the Sabbatarians had come to see the third message as a continuation of the messages of the first two angels, thus making the Sabbatarian Adventists the true heirs of the Millerites. Although not understood at the time, the imperatives of Revelation 14 would eventually lead the Sabbatarians to open their missiological door ever more widely.[14]

Phase II: A Partially Opened Door (1850-1874)

By the early 1850s the shut door on Adventist missions may have opened some, but it had not opened very far. It would be nearly a quarter of a century before the Seventh-day Adventists would send their first overseas missionary. Meanwhile, the incipient denomination's approach to missions moved with the speed of evolution rather than with that of revolution.

Ellen White had indicated in 1848 that the Sabbatarian Adventist message would become as " 'streams of light that went clear round the world,' " and in 1853 that "we are now having the last message of mercy that is ever to be given to a guilty world," but throughout the 1850s her statements were not understood.[15] For example, some questioned the propriety of sending missionaries to foreign lands when there were so many heathen in the United States. Others believed it to be a poor commentary on the "religion of Jesus" for churches to have "a great regard for the heathen—'provided they are *a great way off*' " There was plenty of poverty and suffering close to home, the argument ran, without worrying about those in other countries.[16]

One would think that these early Adventists, so intent on the second coming, would have been inspired to "preach the gospel in all the world" that the end might come. But having accepted the Millerite interpretation of Matthew 24:14, they believed that the gospel had already been preached as a "witness among all nations" and that the prophecy of verse 14 had been fulfilled already.[17] Holding that belief, the Sabbatarian Adventists understandably had little burden for overseas mission work.

In a similar manner, the Sabbatarians had no conviction to take their distinctive message of the second coming to all the world as indicated in the message of the first angel of Revelation 14:6, since they held that the Millerites had accomplished that task prior to 1844. The Millerite method had been to send their publications on ships to the seaports of the world. Thus, by the summer of 1842, Joshua V. Himes could write that Millerite literature had been "sent to all the Missionary stations that we know of on the globe."[18]

Not all Sabbatarian Adventists were satisfied with the "no responsibility" for missions position. Foremost among that group were Joseph Bates and James White—two of their most prominent leaders. In 1855 Bates encouraged his fellow believers to ship literature to Christian mission stations outside of the United States. The next year, White wrote that "a missionary spirit should be cherished by those who profess the Message. Not to send the gospel to the heathen; but to extend the solemn warning throughout the realms of corrupted Christianity."[19]

A second group that not only advocated but became active in foreign missionary work were European immigrants who had been converted to Sabbatarian Adventism in the United States. Literature was translated to reach them in the mid 1850s. A natural reaction was for them to send such literature to their relatives and friends back home. Thus the third angel's message was being preached silently in Europe, and by the early 1860s overseas converts were beginning to make themselves known to the Adventists in America.[20]

Another solution to the "missionary problem" was set forth by Uriah Smith in 1859. The delay of the eschaton was leading some to question

Sabbatarian Adventist missiology. One *Review* reader inquired: "Is the Third Angel's Message being given, or to be given except in the United States?" Smith replied that even though analogy might lead to the conclusion that the proclamation of the third angel's message might be coextensive with the preaching of the first angel (i.e., worldwide), "this might not perhaps be necessary to fulfill Rev. X.11, since our own land is composed of people from almost every nation." Smith's rationale, borrowed from William Miller, was that the gospel merely needed to be preached to a *representative* from each nation. Since the United States was a conglomerate of representative individuals from many nations, foreign missions might not be necessary.[21]

It is impossible to determine how many Sabbatarian Adventists held Smith's North American interpretation of Matthew 24:14 and Revelation 10:11, but that information makes little difference, because the denomination was once again compelled to widen its missiological horizons for the same reason it had earlier been forced to reinterpret its views on the shut door.

This time the issue was forced by the unexpected acquisition of overseas converts as a result of literature distribution by immigrants and others. The American Adventists had been aware of converts in Ireland and England in the early 1860s. And by 1864 there were at least two believers of the third angel's message in Africa, and one of those would soon take the message to Australia.[22]

Whether it liked it or not, the newly-organized Seventh-day Adventist Church was being faced with the challenge of worldwide mission. Not only were there converts, but the converts were calling for missionaries to be sent to their lands.

As on so many other occasions, James White was at the forefront of those who envisioned a larger work for the denomination. A month before the organization of the General Conference of Seventh-day Adventists in April 1863, White wrote in the *Review* that "ours is a world-wide message." A few months before he had pointed out the need for sending a missionary to Europe. Then, in June 1863, the *Review* reported that "the General Conference Executive Committee may send him [B. F. Snook] a missionary to Europe before the close of 1863."[23]

While the newly-established General Conference did not have the manpower to spare to send Snook overseas, it did have a minister who was more than anxious to make the trip. In 1858 Michael Belina Czechowski (an ex-Roman Catholic Polish priest who had converted to Sabbatarian Adventism in America in 1857) wrote: "How I would love to visit my own native country across the big waters, and tell them all about Jesus' coming, and the glorious restitution, and how they must keep the Commandments of God and the Faith of Jesus."[24] Because of the newness of his faith, perceived personal instabilities, and other reasons, the Seventh-day Adventist Church leaders refused to send Czechowski as a missionary.

In frustration, the creative Pole requested and received missionary sponsorship from the Advent Christian denomination (the main body of Millerites). After arriving in Europe in 1864, Czechowski preached the third angel's message of the Seventh-day Adventists in spite of his Advent Christian sponsorship. He promoted his views through public evangelism, publishing a paper (*L'Evangile Eternel*), and the preparation and circulation of tracts. The results of the work of this effective but erratic preacher were the planting of Seventh-day Adventist doctrinal seeds in Switzerland, Italy, Hungary, Romania, and other parts of Europe.[25]

Meanwhile, the Seventh-day Adventists in America (still reluctant missionaries at best) took the "adventurous" step of sending John N. Loughborough and D. T. Bourdeau to California in 1868 in response to a plea from Adventists in that state that a minister be sent.[26] A year later, however, Czechowski's European converts made a move that forced the hesitant American church to expand its missiological understandings and practices.

The occasion for the new mission agitation was contact from Czechowski's followers in Switzerland, who had accidentally discovered the existence of the Seventh-day Adventist Church in the United States—a discovery that upset their leader. Correspondence eventually led the American Adventist leadership to invite a Swiss representative to the 1869 General Conference session. James Erzberger arrived too late to attend the session, but he remained in the Unites States for more than a year to become better grounded in Adventist beliefs. He returned to Europe in 1870 as an ordained Seventh-day Adventist minister.[27]

Notwithstanding Erzberger's failure to arrive in time for the 1869 General Conference session, contact with the European Adventists had stimulated the promotion of a missionary society. "The object of this society," read the action that created it, "shall be to send the truths of the Third Angel's Message to foreign lands, and to distant parts of our own country, by means of missionaries, papers, books, tracts, &c." In introducing the society, James White noted that the church was receiving "almost daily applications to send publications to other lands."[28]

A few months later, J. N. Andrews penned: "We cannot refrain from acknowledging our backwardness" in reaching out to the European Adventists. He indicated that Czechowski's mission was in God's providence.[29] In January 1870 Andrews conceded "the hand of God" in Czechowski's work, noting "that in consequence of our fears to trust money with Bro. Czechowski, and our lack of care to patiently counsel him as to its proper use, God used our most decided opponents to carry forward the work."[30]

In December 1871 the General Conference session voted a resolution concerning God's providence in opening the work in Europe. That resolution further pledged the denomination to "do what lies in our power to assist in the spread of the truth in that country [Switzerland] and in other countries of Europe."[31]

Meanwhile, Ellen White did her part to encourage the denomination's missionary outreach. In December 1871 she had a vision in which she was shown that the Seventh-day Adventists had "truths of vital importance" that were "to test the world." Thus young Adventist men should qualify themselves in "other languages, that God may use them as mediums to communicate His saving truth to those of other nations." Not only was the denomination to send its publications to foreign peoples, but "living preachers" should be sent. "Missionaries," she asserted, "are needed to go to other nations to preach the truth in a guarded, careful manner." The Adventist "message of warning" was to "go to all nations" that they might be tested by the light of its truth. "We have not one moment to lose," she penned. "If we have been careless in this matter, it is high time we were now in earnest to redeem the time, lest the blood of souls be found on our garments."[32]

In spite of the fact that some leading Adventist ministers were still preaching as late as 1872 that the taking of the gospel to all the world referred to in Matthew 24:14 had been essentially fulfilled,[33] the momentum for foreign missions continued to gain force among Seventh-day Adventists. A perennial problem, however, was the lack of educated workers who could be sent. That problem led to moves in 1873 and 1874 toward founding the denomination's first college.[34]

By the summer of 1873 James White was not only calling for a college, but he was urging that J. N. Andrews be sent to Switzerland that autumn in answer to the call for a missionary from the Swiss Adventists.[35] That November saw White call a special session of the General Conference to discuss the sending of a missionary to Switzerland. But in spite of his urging, nothing was done to carry out his desire to send Andrews or anyone else.[36]

It is significant that White's featured sermon at the November 1873 session was an exposition of Revelation 10 in connection with foreign missions. Earlier in the year he had applied the imperative of Revelation 14:6 to preach the everlasting gospel to all the world and the command of Revelation 10:11 to "prophesy again before many peoples, and nations, and tongues, and kings" to the worldwide commission of the Seventh-day Adventist Church in the wake of the Millerite disappointment.[37] Those two texts, along with Matthew 24:14, would eventually impel Adventists missions to every corner of the earth as the denomination sought to fulfill what it saw as its prophetic role in history.

In January 1874 White established the *True Missionary*, Adventism's first missionary journal. Its pages urged the sending of foreign missionaries.

Ellen White shared the broadened vision of her husband. In April 1874 she had an "impressive dream" that helped overcome the remaining Adventist opposition to foreign missions. The "messenger" in her dream provided the following instruction for the reluctant Adventist leaders:

> "You are entertaining too limited ideas of the work for this time. . . . You must take broader views. . . . Your house is the world. . . .
> ". . . The message will go in power to all parts of the world, to Oregon, to Europe, to Australia, to the islands of the sea, to all nations, tongues, and peoples."

She "was shown" that the mission work was far more extensive "than our people have imagined, or even contemplated and planned." As a result, she called for a larger faith to be expressed in action.[38]

That August the General Conference voted that Andrews should go to Europe "as soon as practicable." A month later he sailed for Switzerland as the first "official" Seventh-day Adventist foreign missionary. Remarking on the appointment, Ellen White claimed that the American Adventists had sent "the ablest man in all our ranks."[39]

P. Gerard Damsteegt has accurately summarized the period between 1850 and 1874 as one of "gradual expansion" of the Adventist view of the missionary task. "It was," writes Damsteegt, "a period of transition from the idea of an imminent Second Advent to a realization that before Christ could return the third angel's message had to be proclaimed world-wide."[40]

By the close of the period, the American Adventists had come to grips with at least part of their missiological responsibility and had sent their first official foreign missionary in response to a deepening interpretation of such passages as Revelation 14:6-12 and Revelation 10:11. However, the sending of Andrews ten years after the arrival of Czechowski in Europe, as Rajmund Dabrowski has pointed out, should more accurately be viewed as the "second stage of Adventist missionary activities in Europe" than the first.[41]

By 1874 Adventists were still reluctant missionaries at best. They still had an inadequate vision of worldwide mission. Their missiology was a growing, dynamic concept that would continue to evolve. Meanwhile, both of their first two periods of mission development were necessary steps in an ongoing process. The first stage (1844-1850) provided time for the building of a doctrinal platform, while the second (1850-1874) allowed for the development of a power base in North America for the support of a foreign mission program. The third stage (1874-1889), which we will examine in the next section, also provided needed development before further outreach could take place.

Phase III: Mission to the Christian ("Protestant") Nations (1874-1889)

"The question has often been asked why Seventh-day Adventists should have chosen Central Europe . . . as the first field for their foreign missionary operations." Such was B. L. Whitney's lead statement in 1886 in the first paragraph of the first Adventist book on foreign missions. Part of the answer, as we have seen, was what B. B. Beach has called "Czechowski's Preparatory Mission,"[42] but a complete answer entails a further look at the development of the denomination's missiology.

Andrews provides us with a crucial insight into Whitney's query in his first letter home after arriving in Europe. He wrote:

> I firmly believe that God has much people in Europe who are ready to obey his holy law, and to reverence his Sabbath, and to wait for his Son from Heaven. I came here to give my life to the proclamation of these sacred truths concerning the near advent of Christ and the observance of God's commandments.[43]

In other words, Andrews believed that his job was to present the distinctive Adventist doctrines to those who were already Christians. His was not a mission of general Christianity to the heathen. Responsibility to the heathen would remain outside the scope of Adventist missiology until the 1890s.

Borge Schantz accurately summarizes the Adventist attitude between 1874 and 1890 when he writes that "mission to non-Christians was approved of and praised" by the Adventists, but "it was regarded as the task that other evangelical missionary societies could take care of. When they had brought people to Christ, the SDAs were committed to bringing them the last warning [i.e., the distinctively Adventist doctrines]."[44] Such a missiology grew out of the Adventists' understanding that they were to call people "out of Babylon" in fulfillment of the commission of the three angels of Revelation 14. With that in mind, it is not surprising that the denomination began its mission work in the heartland of Christian Europe.

The sending of letters and literature by American immigrants and other Adventists and the work of Czechowski had laid the groundwork for the Adventist approach to missions in the 1870s and 1880s. In the fall of 1874 S. N. Haskell noted that it had once required "a great stretch of faith to believe this work would find its way to every nation, kindred, tongue, and people, and lead thousands of persons of different nationalities to embrace the Sabbath of the Lord and kindred truths." But, he pointed out, that is what had happened. Hearts had been prepared for the reception of the truth. "Within twenty-five years," Haskell penned, we have seen Adventism "rise from poverty and a very small beginning, gradually increase in strength and power, until its sacred rays are welcomed by individuals all over the world."[45]

It was into the fertile Christian soil of Europe that Adventism placed its first foreign missions. Upon arriving in Switzerland, Andrews found several small congregations of Sabbathkeeping Adventists already in existence—the work of Czechowski and Erzberger. Andrews more fully indoctrinated those believers during his first meetings with them. Beyond that, within two months of his arrival Andrews had heard of congregations of believers in Prussia and Russia and had become convinced "that there are Sabbath-keeping [sic] Christians in most of the countries in Europe." His plan was to develop those already-existing core groups.[46] He hoped to reach them by advertising his desire to correspond with them "in the most widely circulated papers of Europe." Surprisingly, that method worked with a fair degree of success.[47]

Within a short time the Seventh-day Adventists had missions in

England, Scandinavia, and Germany, as well as in Switzerland. From those bases the Adventist message soon spread to other European nations. The missionaries manning these new missions were often returning first-generation European immigrants who had been converted to Adventism in the United States and had been encouraged to return to their native countries. These returning nationals had the advantage of knowing the language and culture and they nearly always had a group of acquaintances with whom to begin their ministry.[48]

By the early 1880s the European mission was reaching the adolescent stage. There were several indications of the mission's growing importance to the denomination. One of those indicators was a series of visits by foremost Adventist leaders sent by the General Conference to tour the various European missions between 1882 and 1887. The first was S. N. Haskell in 1882. Haskell recommended the publication of literature in additional languages and helped the Europeans develop a more functional organizational structure. More important, however, were the visits of G. I. Butler (president of the General Conference) in 1884 and of Ellen G. White and her son (W. C. White) from 1885 through 1887. Such visits not only strengthened the work in Europe, they demonstrated the denomination's interest in its mission work.[49]

A second set of indicators regarding the growing maturation of the European mission was organizational developments. Foremost among these was the first general meeting of workers from the different Seventh-day Adventist missions in Europe in 1882 "for consultation concerning the general wants of the cause." This was the first session of what subsequently became known as the European Council of Seventh-day Adventists. Closely related to the development of the Council was the commencement of publication of German, Italian, and Romanian periodicals in 1884. (The denomination had had a European-based French periodical since 1876.) Another sign of organizational adolescence was the felt need to develop educational institutions to train church workers. That issue was a major item of discussion at the 1884 session of the European Council.[50]

Outside of the European missions, the Adventists established General Conference-sponsored missions among the European Protestants of Australia in 1885 and of South Africa in 1887. Both of these countries had had lay members prior to the arrival of official missionaries. Both would also become home bases (along with America and Europe) for the next phase of Adventist mission development—the taking of the three angels' messages to every nation throughout the world. That phase, beginning about 1889, was the logical outcome of the developing Adventist interpretation of the to-every-kindred-tongue-and-people passages of Revelation 14:6, Revelation 10:11, and Matthew 24:14. By 1889 Adventism was in a position to undertake that larger task; its three prior stages of mission development having prepared a series of firm foundations.

"The Antimission (shut-door) Period" (1844-1850) had allowed for the development of a doctrinal base; the "Partially Opened Door Period" (1850-1874) had afforded time for the building of a power base in North America for the support of missions to other Protestant nations; and the "Mission to the Christian ("Protestant") Nations Period" (1874-1889) had provided for similar development in England, Europe, Australia, and South Africa. Even though much development still needed to take place in each of those mission home bases after 1890, the groundwork had been laid and Adventism was poised to explode into a truly worldwide church as it entered the 1890s.

Phase IV: Mission to the World (1890-1960s)

The early 1890s was an excellent time to be poised in readiness for mission, since that decade would witness one of the greatest expansions of mission in the history of Christianity. Sydney Ahlstrom, a leading student of American church history, has noted that "the closing two decades of the nineteenth century witnessed the climactic phase of the foreign missions movement in American Protestantism."[51]

One of the main stimulants of this interest was the Student Volunteer Movement for Foreign Missions, which grew out of an appeal by Dwight L. Moody in 1886 for college students to devote their lives to mission service. One hundred took their stand. That number increased to 2,200 in 1887, and within a few years many thousands of young people had pledged their lives to mission service. The movement's thrust was that "all should go to all," and its motto was "the evangelization of the world in this generation."[52] The movement stimulated, claims Ernest R. Sandeen, "the greatest demonstration of missionary interest ever known in the United States."[53] As a result, American Protestants began to see such places as India, Africa, China, and Japan as their spiritual provinces.

The continental European nations also witnessed an upsurge of missionary interest and involvement at about the same time that it was experienced in the Anglo-American sphere. Scandinavia, Germany, France, Switzerland, and Holland each had its own student movements for foreign missions. The 1890s was a great decade for Protestant missions.[54]

The dynamic thrust of Protestant, and particularly Anglo-American, missions in the 1890s was of crucial importance to Adventism, especially since the denomination was dominated by Americans and was heavily influenced by developments in the Anglo-American sphere. Thus, just as the foreign-mission movement was picking up speed, Seventh-day Adventism began to take a larger interest in its own missiological role in the world.

The Adventists published their first book on foreign missions— *Historical Sketches of the Foreign Missions of the Seventh-day Adventists*— the same year (1886) that Moody stimulated the birth of the Student Volunteer Movement. Then in early 1889 the denomination sent S. N. Haskell and Percy T. Magan on a two-year itinerary around the world to survey the opportunities, problems, and possible mission sites that awaited Adventist missions in various parts of Africa, India, and the Orient. Their tour was fully reported to the church through the pages of *The Youth's Instructor*.[55] Thus missions and mission service began to capture the hearts and minds of Adventist youth in a manner similar to the way the student movement was affecting thousands of young people in the larger Protestant world.

In November 1889 the General Conference session took the momentous step of creating the Seventh-day Adventist Foreign Mission Board "for the management of the foreign mission work" of the denomination.[56] The same year saw the *Home Missionary* developed as a periodical aimed at promoting the various aspects of missionary work.

The creation of the Foreign Mission Board was more than symbolic. It was an action that proclaimed that Adventists were at last ready to take their mission mandate seriously. Never again would Seventh-day Adventists be backward about foreign missions. To the contrary, they would become known for their exertions to reach the entire world with their peculiar message of the three angels; spreading not only their message but their publishing, medical, and educational institutions wherever they went.

By the end of the 1890s Adventism had been established on every continent and on many of the islands of the sea. In this fourth period of Adventist mission the denomination aimed to reach the "heathen" and Catholics as well as the world's Protestants, even though Adventists usually began their work in even non-Christian countries among the islands of Protestants in those lands.

The rapid growth in worldwide Adventist mission that had begun in the 1890s continued unabated into the twentieth century. It is difficult to grasp the magnitude of the changes in Adventist mission outreach in the early decades of the century, but a graph indicating the increasing number of Adventist missions will help us gain some appreciation of an expansionary move that was beginning to transform the denomination from a North American church into a worldwide movement.

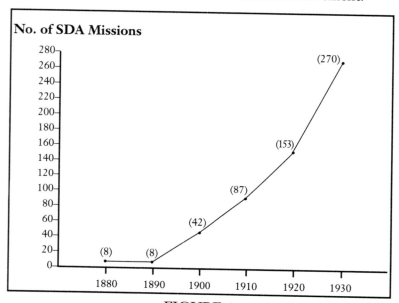

FIGURE 1

Expansion of SDA Missions

A glance at figure 1 indicates several things. One is the lack of mission development before the 1890s. A second is the crucial importance of the 1890s as the decade in which Adventism came to understand its worldwide mission and determined to carry out that mission. The third thing to note is that this understanding and determination did not burn itself out in the 1890s.

The continuous expansion of Adventism into all the world not only changed the geographical boundaries of the church, increasingly it changed the nature of Adventism itself. Table 1 helps us come to grips with some important aspects of that transformation.

An examination of table 1 indicates continuous growth and the fact that the 1890s and 1920s are of special interest. The 1890s, as we noted above, was the decade in which the church began to preach its judgment hour message as "a witness unto all nations." In the mid-1920s the denomination

TABLE 1
Growth of SDA Church by Decades

Year	Evang. Workers North America	Evang. Workers Outside North America	Churches North America	Churches Outside North America	Membership North America	Membership Outside North America
1863	30	——	125	——	3,500	——
1870	72	——	179	——	5,440	40
1880	255	5	615	25	14,984	586
1890	355	56	930	86	27,031	2,680
1900	1,019	481	1,554	338	63,335	12,432
1910	2,326	2,020	1,917	852	66,294	38,232
1920	2,619	4,336	2,217	2,324	95,877	89,573
1930	2,509	8,479	2,227	4,514	120,560	193,693
1940	3,001	10,578	2,624	6,300	185,788	318,964
1950	5,588	12,371	2,878	7,359	250,939	505,773

passed the point where there were more members outside of North America than there were inside. Thus the church was not only preaching worldwide but was beginning to become internationalized.

Some of the implications for internationalization were already becoming clear by the turn of the century. One was an expansion of home bases for the sending of foreign missionaries. While that concept was practiced in the nineteenth century, General Conference President A. G. Daniells consciously sought to further develop Adventism in such nations as Germany, England, and Australia in the early twentieth century, so that they would become even stronger home bases for further expansion.

The early decades of the twentieth century witnessed the German church under the leadership of Louis R. Conradi pioneer the Adventist work in the Middle East and East Africa. Australian missionaries, meanwhile, rapidly spread the message throughout much of the South Pacific. British Adventism, with its nation's global empire and strongly developed missionary tradition, rapidly moved to plant Adventism in many parts of the world. As the century progressed, more and more missions in both developed and undeveloped nations became self-sustaining conferences that could function as home bases for additional mission outreach.

Adventism, of course, took its medical, educational, and publishing work almost everywhere it went. The denomination's institutional base expanded in proportion to the spread of the church itself.[57]

By mid-twentieth century the Seventh-day Adventist Church had work in the vast majority of nations. The denomination was almost unrecognizable from the largely North American church it had been in the 1880s. But the second half of the century would see further transformations that would once again radically change both Adventism's profile and its approach to mission outreach.

Phase V: Mission With Conscious Intent (1960s-present)

In terms of Adventism's changing mission profile, several things should be noted. First, since the mid-twentieth century Adventism has experienced rapid growth in terms of the sheer number of adherents. From a membership of 756,712 in 1950 and 1,245,125 in 1960, the denomination has grown to over 8,000,000 adherents in 1994.

Perhaps more important than the numbers themselves is the fact that an increasing proportion of the Adventist membership resides outside of North America. The most impressive way to demonstrate the internationalization of Adventism is graphically. Figure 2 demonstrates that what was once a North American religion has become a worldwide movement with only a small fraction of its membership in the North American Division.

The demographic shifts illustrated by figure 2 have impacted on the church's understanding of mission in several ways. One has been a developing reciprocity in the sending of "missionaries" between divisions. Whereas a few years ago being a missionary meant going as a

FIGURE 2
Distribution of SDA Membership in Relation to
North America

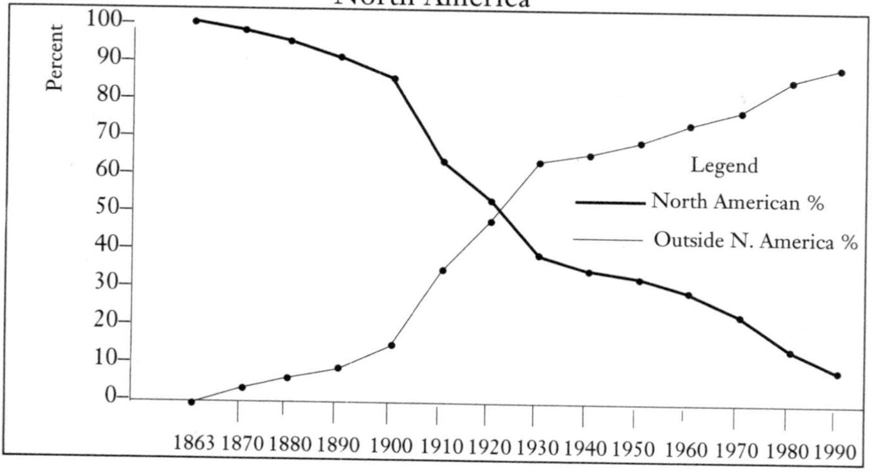

European or North American to some "heathen," non-Christian, or non-Protestant land that might be quite primitive, being a missionary in the 1990s means serving in a place other than one's native land. Thus Africa, Asia, India, and Latin America send "missionaries" to Europe and the United States and even to each other. Of course, Europeans, Australians, Britons, and Americans still serve in other nations, but it is much more a two-way street than it used to be.

"From everywhere to everywhere" has become a familiar phrase in Adventist mission terminology in the 1990s. Since the mission of the church is now viewed in global terms, and since people from around the world serve in other countries, the term *interdivisional worker* more aptly describes people who labor for the church in areas other than their nation of origin than does the word *missionary*.

Another aspect of internationalization and the changing profile of Adventist mission since mid-century is the matter of administrative control. "Foreign missionaries" from the United States, Europe, Great Britain, Australia, and South Africa no longer control the work in the newer fields of Adventist labor. Rather, the church has developed indigenous leaders in nearly every area of its far-flung mission program.

The change from "missionary" to indigenous leadership was stimulated to some extent by the dislocations occasioned by World War II. But the process was speeded up immensely by the spirit of nationalism that spread throughout the world between 1945 and the late 1960s. As a result, the administrators of geographical sectors of Adventism up through the General Conference divisions generally are indigenous to the regions they administrate. That means that the work in India is directed by Indians, the work in Africa by Africans, and the work in South and Central America by Latin Americans. The leader of each world division is also a vice-president of the General Conference. Beyond that, some of the most important positions in the General Conference's central administration are held by leaders from parts of the world that only a few years ago were still dependent on North American and European leadership.

Beyond Adventism's transformed demographic profile since mid-century is its new, more pro-active approach to mission outreach. In its earlier phases, Adventist mission outreach was quite haphazard. Having begun with an antimission philosophy, Adventism later allowed the direction of its mission development to follow the lead of those in other lands who had read Adventist literature and had asked the denomination to send workers. In other words, there was no conscious plan of action to evangelize the world systematically.

That began to change in the 1890s and the first half of the twentieth century, but a major shift toward conscious intent took place when the Department of World Mission and the Seventh-day Adventist Institute of World Mission were added to the Theological Seminary at Andrews University in 1966. The new department taught classes in mission, while the Institute prepared men and women for cross-cultural service through periodically holding special sessions for new mission appointees. Other functions of the Institute have included research and publication on many different aspects of mission and church growth, providing consulting services on mission outreach, and the planning and conducting of seminars and workshops on mission and growth across cultures.

One of the most conspicuous outgrowths of the heightened consciousness of the need to plan systematically for world mission was launched at the 1990 General Conference session as Global Mission.

Global Mission marks a conscious shift in Adventist missiology as the denomination seeks to complete its mission of preaching the three angels' messages "to every nation, and kindred, and tongue, and people" (Rev. 14:6). Adventism has traditionally gauged its mission outreach progress on the "nations" and "tongues" parts of that text. Thus the denomination's statistical reports emphasized that the Adventist church had established work in so many nations and languages. That looked encouraging, because by 1990 the number of people in the small, unentered nations came only to some 94,000,000.

Global Mission, however, has shifted the denomination's eyes away from those comfortable statistics and toward a new way of looking at denominational mission accountability. Rather than focusing on *nations*, Global Mission focuses attention on the fact that the Adventist message is to go to "every *kindred*, and *tongue*, and *people*." That approach is much less comforting.

Research tells us that there are some 5,257 ethno-linguistic or population groupings of roughly one million people each on the planet. As of 1990, Adventists had at least one church in about 3,000 of those groups. That left more than 2,000 in which the denomination had absolutely no presence. Those unentered groupings represented more than two billion people.

Facing such facts, the Adventist church at its 1990 General Conference session felt impelled to open its eyes to the magnitude of the task that lay before it. It has been forced to think of the denomination's task in terms of the most difficult areas to reach, not just those that have been receptive.

The goal of the Global Mission program instituted in 1990 is "to establish an Adventist presence in each" of the "untouched groups of 1 million people before A.D. 2000. *That means planting at least one new church every other day in these unreached areas during the next 10 years!*"[58]

While the Global Mission program has fallen short of its extremely ambitious goals, it has made significant progress. As of the end of 1993, 179 of the previously unreached population segments had been entered by the denomination (as opposed to 83 at the end of 1992) since 1990. Beyond that, by the end of 1993 some 380 additional segments had Global Mission activity in progress.[59]

At the forefront of the initiative to enter the more difficult population segments for evangelization are such official church entities as Adventist World Radio, which seeks to blanket the earth with the message of the three angels, and the Adventist Development and Relief Agency (ADRA), which often finds entry to new areas where more traditional lines of church work are excluded.

Beyond the official outreach programs, the 1980s saw the rise of such independent Adventist mission agencies as Adventist Frontier Missions. The aim of Adventist Frontier Missions is strictly to establish an Adventist presence in unentered areas.

Recent years have also seen more and more short-term and "unofficial" workers enter the ranks of Adventist foreign missions. These missionaries range from students, retirees, and professional volunteers to tentmakers. The tentmaker program recruits people to go as entrepreneurs or as employees of international corporations to establish an Adventist presence and work in unentered areas. Tentmakers are not paid by the church, but they are trained by the church and networked in it.

The Institute of World Mission, under the direction of the Secretariat of the General Conference, is playing an increasing role in the training of tentmakers and short-term missionaries and in generating enthusiasm for mission among young Adventists. The General Conference has also established the Office of Global Mission to oversee the planning for work in unentered areas.

In Perspective

Seventh-day Adventists did not become a missionary people by any conscious design. Nineteenth-century Adventists, points out Borge Schantz, had no "world strategy developed at headquarters" for taking the three angels' messages to the world.[60] Rather, throughout the nineteenth century Adventism had been pushed from one missiological stage to the next by converts who called for missionaries.

Each stage in the denomination's missiological evolution, however, was crucial to its healthy development. Its antimission period (1844-1850) gave Adventism the space to develop a doctrinal identity and to consolidate its membership, its preach-to-those-in-America stage (1850-1874) gave the young denomination time to build a support base for its first overseas missionary endeavors, and its mission-to-the-Protestants stage (1874-1889) allowed it to develop support bases in several strategically-located nations that would supply funds and personnel for Adventism's great thrust into worldwide mission in the 1890s.

The period between the 1890s and the 1960s saw Adventism become an international movement reaching to every corner of the globe. But perhaps the most challenging stage of Adventist mission development has begun to take place in the last few years as Adventism has consciously wrestled with its responsibility to preach the message of the three angels to those areas of the earth that are the most difficult to reach with the Christian message.

The shape of Adventist mission has changed over the years, but the goal has remained the same: to preach God's last-day message to all the world that the end might come (see Revelation 14:6-12; 10:11; Matthew 24:14).

1. The statistics are from the *131st Annual Statistical Report—1993* (Silver Spring, Md.: General Conference of Seventh-day Adventists, 1994), 40, 45. There is no comprehensive history of Seventh-day Adventist mission development, even for the nineteenth century. However, many of the topics covered in this chapter are treated more fully in William A. Spicer, *Our Story of Missions* (Mountain View, Calif.: Pacific Press, 1921); Gottfried Oosterwal, *Mission Possible: The Challenge of Mission Today* (Nashville, Tenn.: Southern Publishing Assn., 1972); P. Gerard Damsteegt, *Foundations of the Seventh-day Adventist Message and Mission* (Grand Rapids, Mich.: Eerdmans, 1977); R. W. Schwarz, *Light Bearers to the Remnant* (Mountain View, Calif.: Pacific Press, 1979); Borge Schantz, "The Development of Seventh-day Adventist Missionary Thought: Contemporary Appraisal" (Ph.D. dissertation, Fuller Theological Seminary, 1983). Beyond these works, George R. Knight, *Anticipating the Advent: A Brief History of Adventism* (Boise, Idaho: Pacific Press, 1993) is written from the perspective of mission development.
2. Helpful treatments of Millerism and the Great Disappointment are found in Damsteegt, *Foundations*; Francis D. Nichol, *The Midnight Cry* (Washington, D.C.: Review and Herald, 1944); David L. Rowe, *Thunder and Trumpets: Millerites and Dissenting Religion in Upstate New York, 1800-1850* (Chico, Calif.: Scholars Press, 1985); Ronald L. Numbers and Jonathan M. Butler, eds., *The Disappointed: Millerism and Millenarianism in the Nineteenth Century* (Bloomington, Ind.: Indiana University Press, 1987); George R. Knight, *Millennial Fever and the End of the World: A Study of Millerite Adventism* (Boise, Idaho: Pacific Press, 1993).
3. William Miller, *Evidence from Scripture and History of the Second Coming of Christ, about the Year 1843* (Boston: Joshua V. Himes, 1842), 237.
4. William Miller, "Letter from Bro. Miller," *Advent Herald*, Dec. 11, 1844, 142.
5. J. H. Waggoner et al., "Conference Address: Organization," *Review and Herald*, June 11, 1861, 21.

6. Ellen G. White to J. N. Loughborough, Aug. 24, 1874.

7. James White, "Repairing the Breach in the Law of God," *Present Truth*, Sept. 1849, 28.

8. Waggoner et al., "Conference Address," *Review and Herald*, June 11, 1861, 21.

9. [James White, editorial note], *Review and Herald*, Apr. 7, 1851, 64. Cf. *Seventh-day Adventist Encyclopedia* (1976 ed.), s.v. "Open and Shut Door."

10. [James White], "The Work of the Lord," *Review and Herald*, May 6, 1852, 4-5.

11. James White, "Call at the Harbinger Office," *Review and Herald*, Feb. 17, 1852, 95.

12. Ellen G. White, *Life Sketches of Ellen G. White* (Mountain View, Calif.: Pacific Press Publishing Assn., 1915), 125.

13. Ellen G. White, "A Vision the Lord Gave Me at Oswego," Unpublished Manuscript, July 29, 1850; Ellen G. White to J. N. Loughborough, Aug. 24, 1874.

14. Joseph Bates, *The Seventh Day Sabbath: A Perpetual Sign* (New Bedford, Mass.: Joseph Bates, 1847 edition), 59; [James White], "The Third Angel's Message," *Present Truth*, Apr. 1850, 65-69; Damsteegt, *Foundations*, 216.

15. E. G. White, *Life Sketches*, 125; Ellen G. White, "To the Saints Scattered Abroad," *Review and Herald*, Feb. 17, 1853, 155.

16. "Civilized Heathen," *Review and Herald*, Aug. 23, 1864, 99; J. H. Waggoner, "The True Field of Missionary Effort," *Review and Herald*, Jan. 13, 1874, 36, 37; [Uriah Smith], "Send the Gospel to the Heathen," *Review and Herald*, Apr. 24, 1856, 11.

17. Damsteegt, *Foundations*, 50-53; "The Gospel of the Kingdom," *Review and Herald*, Mar. 21, 1854, 70.

18. Joshua V. Himes, "The Crisis Has Come!," *Signs of the Times*, Aug. 3, 1842, 140. Cf. Schwarz, *Light Bearers*, 24-30.

19. Joseph Bates, "From Bro. Bates," *Review and Herald*, May 29, 1855, 240; James White, "The Third Angel's Message," *Review and Herald*, Sept. 4, 1856, 141. The church would eventually adopt White's approach, at least up through 1890.

20. Schantz, "Development," 244, 245.

21. "Letters," *Review and Herald*, Feb. 3, 1859, 87. Cf. [Uriah Smith, editorial comment], *Review and Herald*, Jan. 1, 1867, 48; [Uriah Smith], "The Gospel Preached in All the World," *Review and Herald*, July 16, 1872, 36; James White, "Our Faith and Hope," *Review and Herald*, Dec. 27, 1870, 9, 10.

22. Damsteegt, *Foundations*, 285-287; Schwarz, *Light Bearers*, 148, 149.

23. [James White], "The Light of the World," *Review and Herald*, Apr. 21, 1863, 165; [James White], "Books to Ireland," *Review and Herald*, Dec. 30, 1862, 40; [James White], "God's Free Men," *Review and Herald*, June 2, 1863, 8.

24. M. B. Czechowski to Ellen G. White, Aug. 29, 1858, in "The French Mission," *Review and Herald*, Sept. 23, 1858, 144.

25. For the most complete treatment of Czechowski, see Rajmund Ladyslaw Dabrowski and B. B. Beach, eds., *Michael Belina Czechowski, 1818-1876* (Warsaw: "Znaki Czasu" Publishing House, 1979). See also, Rajmund Ladyslaw Dabrowski, "The Forerunner: M. B. Czechowski," in *J. N. Andrews: The Man and the Mission*, Harry Leonard, ed. (Berrien Springs, Mich.: Andrews University Press, 1985), 190-201.

26. Harold Oliver McCumber, *Pioneering the Message in the Golden West* (Mountain View, Calif.: Pacific Press, 1946), 58-70.

27. Schwarz, *Light Bearers*, 143, 144.

28. James White, "Seventh-day Adventist Missionary Society," *Review and Herald*, June 15, 1869, 197.

29. [J. N. Andrews], "The Seventh-day Adventists of Europe," *Review and Herald*, Nov. 30, 1869, 181.

30. [J. N. Andrews], "Cause in Switzerland," *Review and Herald*, Jan. 11, 1870, 22.

31. James White, "Business Proceedings of the Tenth Annual Session of the General Conference of Seventh-day Adventists," *Review and Herald*, Jan. 2, 1872, 20.

32. E. G. White, *Life Sketches*, 203-207.

33. E.g., Dudley Canright, "Present Condition of the World," *Review and Herald*, Apr. 16, 1872, 138.

34. See Emmett K. Vande Vere, *The Wisdom Seekers* (Nashville, Tenn.: Southern Publishing Assn., 1972); George R. Knight, ed., *Early Adventist Educators* (Berrien Springs, Mich.: Andrews University Press, 1983), 11-94.

35. James White, "Progress of the Cause," *Review and Herald*, Aug. 26, 1873, 84.

36. G. I. Butler and Uriah Smith, "Business Proceedings of the Twelfth Annual Meeting of the S.D.A. General Conference," *Review and Herald*, Nov. 25, 1873, 190.

37. James White, "Conference Address before the General Conference of the S. D. Adventists, March 11, 1873," *Review and Herald*, May 20, 1873, 180.

38. E. G. White, *Life Sketches*, 208-210. Cf. Ellen G. White, *Testimonies for the Church* (Mountain View, Calif.: Pacific Press, 1948), 7:34-36.

39. G. I. Butler and Sidney Brownsberger, "Proceedings of the Thirteenth Annual Meeting of the Gen. Conf. of S. D. Adventists," *Review and Herald*, Aug. 25, 1874, 75; E. G. White to Brethren in Switzerland, Aug. 29, 1878.

40. Damsteegt, *Foundations*, 292.

41. Dabrowski, "The Forerunner," 198.

42. B. L. Whitney, "The Central European Mission," in *Historical Sketches of the Foreign Missions of the Seventh-day Adventists* (Basel: Imprimerie Polyglotte, 1886), 9; B. B. Beach, "M. B. Czechowski—Trailblazer for the J. N. Andrews Central European Mission," in Dabrowski, *Czechowski*, 426.

43. J. N. Andrews, "Our Arrival in Switzerland," *Review and Herald*, Nov. 17, 1874, 166.

44. Schantz, "Development," 252, 253. Cf. Oosterwal, *Mission*, 27, 28, 37, 38.

45. S. N. Haskell, "To Nations, Tongues, and People," *Review and Herald*, Nov. 10, 1874, 157.

46. J. N. Andrews, "Meeting of the Sabbath-keepers in Neuchatel," *Review and Herald*, Nov. 24, 1874, 172; J. N. Andrews, "Sabbath-keepers in Prussia," *Review and Herald*, Nov. 24, 1874, 172.

47. J. N. Andrews, "The Work in Europe," *Review and Herald*, Jan. 28, 1875, 36; Mar. 18, 1875, 93.

48. Schantz, "Development," 261, 262.

49. Whitney, "Central European Mission," 37, 43, 51; Arthur L. White, *Ellen G. White: The Lonely Years, 1876-1891* (Washington, D.C.: Review and Herald, 1984), 287-373.

50. Whitney, "Central European Mission," 38, 39, 45, 42, 24, 55, 56; "Report of Missionary Councils," in *Historical Sketches*, 109, 110.

51. Sydney E. Ahlstrom, *A Religious History of the American People* (New Haven, Conn.: Yale University Press, 1972), 864.

52. John R. Mott, "Report of the Executive Committee," in *Student Mission Power: Report of the First International Convention of the Student Volunteer Movement for Foreign Missions, Held at Cleveland, Ohio, U.S.A., February 26, 27, 28 and March 1, 1891* (Pasadena, Calif.: William Carey Library, 1979), 21-23, 38; Kenneth Scott Latourette, *A History of the Expansion of Christianity*, vol 4: *The Great Century in Europe and the United States of America* (Grand Rapids, Mich.: Zondervan, 1970), 97.

53. Ernest R. Sandeen, *The Roots of Fundamentalism: British and American Millenarianism, 1800-1930* (Grand Rapids, Mich.: Baker, 1978), 183.

54. Latourette, *Great Century*, 98.

55. Ella M. Robinson, *S. N. Haskell: Man of Action* (Washington, D.C.: Review and Herald, 1967), 95-125.

56. "General Conference Proceedings: Seventeenth Meeting," *General Conference Bulletin*, 1889, 141, 142.

57. See chapter 6 for the spread of Adventism's institutional support structure throughout the world.

58. Neal Wilson, in "Global Mission: Person to Person," 3. An insert in the *Adventist Review* of July 5, 1990.

59. *131st Annual Statistical Report—1993*, 39, 40.

60. Schantz, "Development," 332.

Chapter 6

Adventism's Missiological Quadrilateral:

A Design for World Mission

As of the mid 1990s the Seventh-day Adventist Church has one of the most far-flung mission enterprises in the history of Christianity. Beginning as a shut-door, antimission people in the 1840s, by the 1890s Adventists had been driven to the conviction that their unique preaching of the three angel's messages of Revelation 14 necessitated that they take their message "to every nation, and kindred, and tongue, and people" (verse 6).

In accomplishing that task they developed a fourfold program of mission outreach that would eventually be exported to all the world. Adventism's fourfold missiological program (its missiological quadrilateral) was pioneered in the Northeastern United States between 1849 and 1874, replicated in the mission to California between the late 1860s and 1882, exported to Europe beginning in 1874, and eventually taken to most nations of the earth.

The Adventist missiological quadrilateral consists of the publishing, medical, educational, and conference aspects of the denomination's work. While the quadrilateral does not seem to have come about by conscious design (anymore than the development of Adventist mission itself), its mature form turned out to be quite congruent with Adventism's wholistic view of human nature and reality in general.

Adventist thought is wholistic in the sense that it sees human nature as a unity, rather than as a series of somewhat separate parts that can be divorced from each other. For example, Adventism has never held that human beings are composed of spirit + soul + body. Rather, they have argued that when God's lifegiving spirit is combined with a functional body a person becomes a unique living soul (see Genesis 2:7). To destroy any part is to destroy the whole. Thus Adventists from the beginning of their movement have argued against those interpretations of hellfire and the state of human beings in death that are based upon Greek dualities of body and soul.[1]

In a similar manner, Adventism at its clear-thinking best avoids all separation of reality into the sacred and the secular. Nothing is secular in the sense that it is separate from God. All of creation and life is sacred because God is the Creator and Sustainer of all that exists.[2]

The missiological corollaries of such a theology lead to a mission program that not only touches the spiritual nature of people, but also seeks to meet their mental and physical needs. Thus the eventual development of the Adventist missiological quadrilateral; a fourfold program to reach the entire person.

The Genesis of the Quadrilateral

The earliest Seventh-day Adventists had no concept of mission. For them the work of warning sinners had been completed. The door of salvation had been shut on October 22, 1844, and their only task was to reach out to other Millerites to convince them of the truths of the heavenly sanctuary, the seventh-day Sabbath, and a few other special beliefs. The Sabbatarian Adventists held that vision of mission for about six or seven years.[3]

But that missiological perspective was destined to frustration and failure. One of the first glimpses of its shortcomings came in a vision that young Ellen G. White had in Dorchester, Massachusetts, in November 1848. After coming out of vision, Ellen said to her husband:

> "I have a message for you. You must begin to print a little paper and send it out to the people. Let it be small at first; but as the people read, they will send you means with which to print, and it will be a success from the first. From this small beginning it was shown to me to be like *streams of light that went clear round the world.*"[4]

In many ways that vision was the genesis of both Adventist publishing and a concept of Adventist mission to the entire world. Not that the "little paper" was the first publishing venture of Sabbatarian Adventists, but it was the first to be continuously sustained.

Because of the Dorchester vision, James White started a periodical entitled *Present Truth*. *Present Truth's* entire aim was one of missionary outreach, even though the concept of mission was extremely restricted. The purpose of the paper was to win other Millerites to an understanding of the seventh-day Sabbath and to the progressive and sequential preaching of the three angels of Revelation 14.[5]

The summer of 1850 saw James begin publishing a second periodical—*The Advent Review*. The purpose of *The Advent Review* was to impress the scattered Millerites with the forcefulness and truthfulness of the 1844 movement through the reprinting of many of the most important Millerite articles of the early 1840s.

November 1850 witnessed the combining of *The Present Truth* and *The Advent Review* into *The Second Advent Review and Sabbath Herald*. That journal, currently known as *The Adventist Review*, truly has become a worldwide periodical that has encircled the world "like streams of light."

For many years the *Review and Herald* was essentially "the church" for most Sabbatarians. After all, they had no church buildings, denomination, or regular congregational preachers. The periodic arrival of the *Review* provided the scattered Adventists with news of their church and fellow believers, sermons, and a sense of belonging.

The regular publication of the *Review and Herald* made it the hub or center of a growing publishing work among Sabbatarians. And that publishing work was the first stage in the development of Adventism's missiological quadrilateral.[6]

The growth of a strong publishing work among Sabbatarian Adventists eventually led to the development of the second stage in Adventism's missiological quadrilateral—church organization. Not only did the publishing work hold the evolving denomination together, but it also, as it obtained more and more property, led to the need for an organization to hold that property. Beyond that, the new organization needed a name so that the publishing organization could be incorporated under the laws of Michigan. Thus we find that the first concrete step in the formation of the Seventh-day Adventist Church as a legal denomination took place with the incorporation of the Seventh-day Adventist Publishing Association on May 3, 1861.[7]

Once that first step in formal organization had taken place, others rapidly followed. In October 1861 the Michigan Conference of Seventh-day Adventists was formed with William A. Higley (a layman) as president. The year 1862 saw the organization of seven more local conferences: Southern Iowa (March 16), Northern Iowa (May 10), Vermont (June 15), Illinois (September 28), Wisconsin (September 28), Minnesota (October 4), and New York (October 25).

The final step in the development of church organization took place at a meeting of representatives of the local conferences at Battle Creek in May 1863. At that time the General Conference of Seventh-day Adventists was formed, with John Byington as its first president.[8]

The 1863 organization served the church until 1901-1903, when the denomination reorganized by adding (1) union conferences to disperse administrative authority and (2) departments (such as educational, publishing, and medical) to better coordinate the various aspects of Adventist outreach.

The point we especially want to note at this time is that Seventh-day Adventist church organization is not based upon any biblical ecclesiology or doctrine of the church. Rather, as the important Ph.D. dissertations of Andrew Mustard and Barry Oliver demonstrate, the organizational developments in the Adventist Church in both 1861-1863 and 1901-1903 took place with functionality of mission outreach in view.[9]

We need to see church or conference organization as the second core element in the Adventist missiological quadrilateral. It is the element, however, that coordinates the outreach of the other three.

The third element in the quadrilateral rapidly followed on the heels of the accomplishment of the second. Just 15 days after the establishment of the General Conference, Ellen White had her first major health reform vision on June 6, 1863. "I saw," she wrote,

> that it was a sacred duty to attend to our health, and arouse others to their duty. . . . We have a duty to speak, to come out against intemperance of every kind,—intemperance in working, in eating, in drinking, and in drugging—and then point them to God's great medicine[:] water, pure soft water, for diseases, for health, for cleanliness, and for . . . luxury. . . .
> I saw that we should not be silent upon the subject of health but should wake up minds to the subject.

In the same document she noted that "the work God requires of us will not shut us away from caring for our health. The more perfect our health, the more perfect will be our labor."[10]

But health reform for Seventh-day Adventists was not just a personal thing. It had social and missiological implications. That became increasingly clear in December 1865, when Ellen White had a second major health reform vision. That vision called for Adventists to establish their own health reform institution.

That institution, according to Ellen White, would have a twofold missiological impact. First, it would affect the lives of Adventist believers by preparing them for "the loud cry of the third angel" through fitting them for translation. Of course, improved health would also prepare believers to be better communicators of their message to others.[11]

A second missiological aspect of the new health institution would be direct outreach to non-Adventists. "As unbelievers," Ellen White penned,

> shall resort to an institution devoted to the successful treatment of disease and conducted by Sabbathkeeping physicians, they will be brought directly under the influence of the truth. By becoming acquainted with our people and our real faith, their prejudice will be overcome and they will be favorably impressed. *By thus being placed under the influence of truth, some will not only obtain relief from bodily infirmities, but will find a healing balm for their sin-sick souls. . . .*
>
> One such precious soul saved will be worth more than all the means needed to establish such an institution.[12]

The December 25, 1865, vision also integrated health reform with Adventist theology, indicating that "the health reform . . . is a part of the third angel's message and is just as closely connected with it as are the arm and hand with the human body."[13]

Some preachers and other Adventist believers must have gotten carried away with enthusiasm for the health-reform message. Thus a few months later Mrs. White carefully corrected any wrong impressions she may have given concerning health reform by writing that "the health reform is closely connected with the work of the third message, yet it is not the message. Our preachers should teach the health reform, yet they should not make this the leading theme in the place of the message." Rather, it had a "preparatory" function as God's people became ready for end-time events.[14]

The institutional fruitage of the 1865 vision was almost immediate.

Ellen White presented the need for an Adventist health institution at the fourth session of the General Conference in May 1866. It soon was decided to establish a health institution in Battle Creek. On September 5, 1866, the Western Health Reform Institute opened under the direction of Dr. Horatio S. Lay, who had served as a physician at the influential water-cure institution at Dansville, New York. Beyond the Western Health Reform Institute, 1866 also saw the development of an Adventist periodical, *The Health Reformer*, to help spread the health message.[15]

The year 1876 witnessed the arrival of twenty-four-year-old John Harvey Kellogg to be chief administrator of the Western Health Reform Institute. Within a few months Kellogg had changed the institution's name to the Battle Creek Sanitarium. The word "sanitarium," he proclaimed, means a "place where people learn to stay well." By the 1890s the Battle Creek Sanitarium had become the largest institution of its kind in the world and had achieved international renown. By that time Adventism's preaching of the gospel had become quite intertwined with the proclamation of the good news of health reform.[16]

The fourth and final aspect of the Adventist missiological quadrilateral took form between 1872 and 1874. That fourth aspect was the denomination's establishment of a college in Battle Creek.

Battle Creek College was not the first attempt at Christian schooling by Adventists, but it was the first sponsored by anything other than a local church. All previous attempts at formal education by Adventists had ended in failure.

But by 1872 a crisis was in the making. In short, the denomination did not have a sufficient supply of preachers. Beyond that, since the 1869 General Conference session there had been rumblings of a foreign mission work. That year Adventist believers in Switzerland (from the work of M. B. Czechowski) had discovered the Adventist church in America and had designated a representative to attend the General Conference meetings. They had also requested that a worker be sent to them.[17]

One result was that the 1869 conference established a missionary society. "The object of this society," read the action that created it, "shall be to send the truths of the Third Angel's Message to foreign lands, and to distant parts of our own country, by means of missionaries, papers, books, tracts, &c." In introducing the society, James White claimed that the church was receiving "almost daily applications to send publications to other lands."[18]

Any such increase in the outreach of the church would not only necessitate ministers, but also translators, editors, and others to engage in additional foreign language printing. Thus needs were building along several lines for the establishment of formal schooling to meet the needs of the church. Those needs were especially felt by James White, who often found himself responsible for the training of young ministers.[19]

His wife was also feeling pressure. In late 1871 Ellen White received a vision indicating a need for more dedication in presenting Adventism to others. Thus she called for young men to learn foreign languages so "that God may use them as mediums to communicate His saving truth to those of other nations." Not only must foreign language publications increase, but, she indicated, men and women must be sent abroad to bear a personal witness.[20]

Then in 1874 two things happened that would forever change the face and very nature of Adventism. First the Battle Creek school (founded in 1872) became Battle Creek College and, second, John Nevins Andrews was sent to Europe as Adventism's first "official" foreign missionary.

It was no accident that the sending of the denomination's first foreign missionary and the establishment of its first college took place the same year. The college was seen as a necessary institution for the training of missionaries for both the homeland and overseas.

Thus Andrews could write in 1873:

> The calls that come from every quarter, from men speaking other languages, must be answered by us. We cannot do this in our present circumstances. But we can do it if the Lord bless our effort in the establishment of our proposed school. We have delayed this effort too long. The time past cannot be recalled, but the time still remaining can be improved. . . . Men of other nationalities desire to be instructed concerning [the second coming].[21]

In a similar vein, General Conference president George I. Butler penned a year later (just before the opening of the college) that

> we see a great work before us to be done. We see the time coming when scores and hundreds of missionaries will go from this land to other lands to sound forth the last message of warning. . . .

... We want hundreds of our people to take three, six, twelve, eighteen, or twenty-four months' schooling, as soon as they can consistently do so.[22]

There was absolutely no doubt in the minds of the founders of Battle Creek College; their educational institution was to have a missiological focus.

Thus by 1874 the last piece of the Adventist missiological quadrilateral was in place. The young denomination had its publishing arm to spread the message, its medical branch to prepare the lives and hearts of people, and its educational work to train workers and nourish young believers. Ideally, all of those aspects of Adventist outreach would be coordinated by the conference system.

Before the nineteenth century was over, the Adventist quadrilateral had been planted on every continent and was making progress in many of the island nations.

Exporting the Quadrilateral to California

The first mission of the Seventh-day Adventist Church outside of the Northeastern United States was to far-off California—a state separated from the rest of the republic by over 1,000 miles of desert, forests, and mountains. The intervening wilderness between the two parts of the nation was not only great in distance, but also difficult (and at times dangerous) to travel.

In the nineteenth century, individual Adventists or denominational literature generally arrived in a locale long before the church had any formal work there. Such was the situation in California. In 1859 M. G. Kellogg and his family had immigrated to San Francisco after a difficult six-month trip across the country by railroad, wagon, and oxcart.[23]

By the early 1860s a company of believers had developed around Kellogg. In 1865 that little group decided to send $133 in gold to Battle Creek to pay the travel expenses of a minister. But, unfortunately, the General Conference had no one to send.[24] The *Review and Herald* continued to be the only link between the believers in the East and those in the West.

Then in 1868 Kellogg attended the General Conference session in Battle Creek and made a personal plea for a minister to be sent to his state. That resulted in John N. Loughborough and D. T. Bourdeau sailing for their new post on June 22, 1868.

Within a short time of their arrival in San Francisco, the two missionaries were met by a man from Petaluma (forty miles to the north) who claimed that a friend had had an impressive dream in which he saw the two tent evangelists and was told to help them.[25] From that providential beginning, the work grew rapidly in California and other areas in the far western United States.

The important point to note is that the California mission replicated the fourfold work of the church in Battle Creek and thus provided a pattern for Adventist missions around the world. Two things should be noted about the establishment of the missiological quadrilateral in California. First, it does not seem to have been intentional in the sense that the pioneer missionaries or the denominational leaders in Battle Creek had sat down and developed a plan of balanced missionary action. After all, by the time the California mission began, the last piece in the quadrilateral—the educational aspect—was still several years from being established in Battle Creek. Thus it seems safe to surmise that the eventual development of the quadrilateral in California grew out of both the example of the Battle Creek experience and the very logic of Adventist wholistic philosophy.

A second thing to note about the development of the quadrilateral in California is that its development took nearly a decade (1873-1882) to complete from the founding of the first element in the quadrilateral to the establishment of the last. That was much quicker than in Battle Creek, where the establishment of the original quadrilateral took a quarter of a century—from 1849 to 1874.

By the end of the century replications of the quadrilateral would take place with even greater rapidity than in California in many new fields. But by then Seventh-day Adventists had a better concept of their mission and how best to achieve it. Beyond that, they had a great deal more experience with the planting of institutions.

Unlike the experience of the denomination in the eastern part of the United States, in the California mission field the conference work—as the organizing arm of the quadrilateral—came first. By 1870 there were more than 100 Sabbath keepers in California. That number had grown to 238 by February 1873, when the California Conference was established with seven churches.[26]

The establishment of the other three parts of the quadrilateral followed the same sequential order as in the East. The fall 1873 camp meeting in Yountville, California, laid plans to establish both a health institute and a branch publishing house.[27] Of those two, the publishing work was the first to see reality. The first issue of *The Signs of the Times* came off the press on June 4, 1874.

"*The Signs of the Times*," wrote James White (its editor), "is designed to be not only an expositor of the prophecies, a reporter of the signs of our times, but also a family, religious, and general news paper for the household." Through the *Signs* the denomination sought to reach the growing population on the Pacific Coast.[28]

The following year (on April 1, 1875) the Pacific Seventh-day Adventist Publishing Association was organized with headquarters in Oakland, California.[29] That institution soon became the Pacific Press Publishing Association. It is still operating in the 1990s, although it has moved to Boise, Idaho.

The next step in the development of the quadrilateral in California came in the summer of 1878, with the establishment of the Rural Health Retreat in the northern part of the state. The final step took place in 1882, with the founding of Healdsburg College a few miles from the Health Retreat. The new school, like its predecessor in the East, was not only to nurture Adventists in the faith but to prepare gospel workers. Today it is known as Pacific Union College.[30]

The Quadrilateral in Europe

About the time that the Adventist missiological quadrilateral received its last contribution in Battle Creek and was barely underway in California, it was also being taken to foreign lands. The first Seventh-day Adventist mission outside of North America was in Switzerland, where a Polish ex-Roman Catholic priest by the name of Michael Belina Czechowski had begun preaching the three angels' messages in 1864.

Czechowski had desired to be sent as a Seventh-day Adventist missionary, but the brethren were not quite ready for such a move; nor did they completely trust their relatively new convert. As a result, the creative Pole requested and received missionary sponsorship from the Advent Christian denomination (the main body of Sunday-keeping Millerites). After arriving in Europe, however, Czechowski preached the Seventh-day Adventist message in spite of his Advent Christian sponsorship.[31]

By the end of the decade he had established a company of believers in Switzerland who had no knowledge that there were Sabbathkeepers in the United States. Late in the 1860s, however, one of Czechowski's converts accidentally discovered the existence of the Seventh-day Adventist Church in the United States through finding a copy of the *Review and Herald* in a room Czechowski had occupied during a recent visit. Subsequent events led to the sending of J. N. Andrews to Switzerland in 1874 to officially establish the work of the church.[32]

As in Battle Creek and California, Andrews and his European colleagues soon began to put the denomination's missiological quadrilateral in place. As usual, the first institutional (as distinct from conference) step in the formation of the quadrilateral was the establishment of a publishing work in Switzerland.

The initial moves were taken about a month after Andrews' arrival in the country, when in mid-November 1874 the Swiss believers "voted to raise the sum of 2000 francs to commence the work of publishing." A Tract and Missionary Society was organized in December 1875 to promote the circulation of Adventist publications. And April 1876 saw the first issue of *Le Signes des Temps* (the French *Signs of the Times*) come off the press.[33]

Meanwhile, another part of the quadrilateral came into place with the organization of the Swiss conference out of the Swiss mission in 1884. The medical work in the form of the "Institut Sanitaire" was begun in 1895, and a school was opened in 1896.[34]

The institutional work in Switzerland was never as strong as it was in the United States, and Switzerland was soon to be overshadowed on the European continent by its German neighbor to the North under the untiring leadership of Louis R. Conradi.[35]

Conradi arrived in Europe in 1886. In 1889 the German church under Conradi's leadership made Hamburg its headquarters. Within the next twelve years the German Adventist church would become the strongest in Europe, with a major printing press in Hamburg, the first European training school for Adventist workers established at Friedensau in 1899, and also a sanitarium at that location.[36]

Comparable national systems featuring the Adventist missiological quadrilateral were soon developed in Great Britain, Scandinavia, and France. Outside of Europe, Australia and South Africa witnessed the development of similar structures in the 1890s.

Replication of the Quadrilateral Around the World

From those home bases and the United States the Adventist quadrilateral was planted in all quarters of the earth in the great mission expansion that began in the 1890s and extended unabated up to the Great Depression of the 1930s. Although slowed down by the depression and World War II, the expansion of Adventism has continued up to the present time. The quadrilateral has continued to be the *modus operandi* of Adventist mission. As a result, statistics of Adventist institutions are impressive.

As of December 31, 1993, the Seventh-day Adventist Church operated 85 colleges and universities, 953 secondary schools, 4,492 primary schools, 148 hospitals and sanitariums, 446 clinics and other medical outreach entities, and 56 publishing houses. Beyond that, the denomination is currently made up of 92 union conferences and missions and 447 local conferences and missions. Its more than 8,000,000 members in 1994 are housed in nearly 40,000 organized congregations.[37]

It should be noted that while the quadrilateral pattern of Adventist missions is the wholistic ideal, it has not always been taken in its fullness everywhere that Adventist missions have permeated. One variable is differing political and social conditions in various geographic areas. Other variables include the needs and opportunities of individual fields of labor. But despite some regional differences, the general pattern remains the same.

The challenge in the 1990s will not be to change the pattern, but to make every effort to keep the various aspects of the missiological model effective for mission. After all, we live in a secularizing world and it is all too easy for such institutional entities as hospitals and colleges to become ends in themselves as they serve the medical and educational needs of their communities. Meeting those needs is good and commendable, but it is not sufficient as a basis for church sponsorship. Beyond contributing to the daily needs of local communities, Adventist institutions must lead men and women into a better understanding of and a stronger relationship to Jesus Christ and the message of the three angels.[38]

In conclusion, religious mission was the reason for the establishment of each sector of the Adventist missiological quadrilateral, and religious mission is the only reason for their continued existence. If that evangelistic mission is kept at the forefront, the Adventist missiological quadrilateral will have a major part in preparing a lost world for the appearance of the Lord of Lords at the end and climax of world history.

---

1. See Robert M. Johnston, "Seventh-day Adventist Church," in Christopher Jay Johnson and Marsha G. McGee, eds., *Encounters With Eternity: Religious Views of Death and Life and Life After-Death* (New York: Philosophical Library, 1986), 277-292; J. R. Zurcher, *The Nature and Destiny of Man: Essay on the Problem of the Union of the Soul and the Body in Relation to the Christian Views of Man,* trans. Mabel R. Bartlett (New York: Philosophical Library, 1969).
2. George R. Knight, *Myths in Adventism: An Interpretative Study of Ellen White, Education, and Related Issues* (Washington, D.C.: Review and Herald, 1985), 127-138.
3. Richard W. Schwarz, *Light Bearers to the Remnant* (Mountain View, Calif.: Pacific Press, 1979), 55, 69, 70; George R. Knight, *Anticipating the Advent: A Brief History of Seventh-day Adventists* (Boise, Idaho: Pacific Press, 1993), 37-39.
4. Ellen G. White, *Life Sketches of Ellen G. White* (Mountain View, Calif.: Pacific Press, 1915), 125. (Italics supplied.)

5. James White, [Prospectus], *The Present Truth*, July 1849, 1; Arthur L. White, *Ellen G. White* (Washington, D.C.: Review and Herald, 1981-1986), 1:163-178.
6. For the history of Adventist publishing see M. Carol Hetzell, *The Undaunted: The Story of the Publishing Work of Seventh-day Adventists* (Mountain View, Calif.: Pacific Press, 1967).
7. *Review and Herald*, May 7, 1861, 200; Andrew G. Mustard, *James White and SDA Organization: Historical Development, 1844-1881* (Berrien Springs, Mich.: Andrews University Press, 1988), 149; *Seventh-day Adventist Encyclopedia* (1976 ed.), s.v. "Publishing Department."
8. *Seventh-day Adventist Encyclopedia* (1976 ed.), s.v. "Organization, Development of, in SDA Church."
9. Mustard, *James White*; Barry David Oliver, *SDA Organizational Structure: Past, Present, and Future* (Berrien Springs, Mich.: Andrews University Press, 1989).
10. Ellen G. White, "Testimony Regarding James and Ellen White, unpublished manuscript, Ms 1, 1863.
11. Ellen G. White, *Testimonies for the Church* (Mountain View, Calif.: Pacific Press, 1948), 1:486.
12. Ibid., 1:493 (emphasis supplied).
13. Ibid., 1:486.
14. Ibid., 1:559.
15. *Seventh-day Adventist Encyclopedia* (1976 ed.), s.v. "Battle Creek Sanitarium"; Dores Eugene Robinson, *The Story of Our Health Message*, 3d ed. (Nashville, Tenn.: Southern Publishing Association, 1955), 144, 145; John Byington and U. Smith, "Fourth Annual Session of General Conference," *Review and Herald*, May 22, 1866, 196; "Prospectus of the *Health Reformer*," *Review and Herald*, June 5, 1866, 8.
16. Richard W. Schwarz, *John Harvey Kellogg, M.D.* (Nashville, Tenn.: Southern Publishing Assn., 1970), 60-62; Richard W. Schwarz, "John Harvey Kellogg, American Health Reformer," Ph.D. dissertation, University of Michigan, 1964, 173-177.
17. Schwarz, *Light Bearers*, 143, 144.
18. James White, "Seventh-day Adventist Missionary Society," *Review and Herald*, June 15, 1869, 197.
19. James White, "Conference Address," *Review and Herald*, May 20, 1873, 180, 181, 184.
20. E. G. White, *Life Sketches*, 203-207.
21. J. N. Andrews, "Our Proposed School," *Review and Herald*, April 1, 1873, 124.
22. George I. Butler, "What Use Shall We Make of Our School?" *Review and Herald*, July 21, 1874, 44, 45.
23. The best published study of the early Adventist work in California is still Harold Oliver McCumber, *Pioneering the Message in the Golden West* (Mountain View, Calif.: Pacific Press, 1946). Revised and reprinted by the same publisher in 1974 as *The Advent Message in the Golden West*.
24. General Conference Committee, "To the Brethren in California," *Review and Herald*, Dec. 11, 1866, 12.
25. McCumber, *Pioneering*, 65, 72.
26. Ibid., 110; *Seventh-day Adventist Encyclopedia* (1976 ed.), s.v. "California Conference."
27. McCumber, *Pioneering*, 113.
28. James White, Editorial, *Signs of the Times*, June 11, 1874, 16.
29. *Seventh-day Adventist Encyclopedia* (1976 ed.), s.v. "Pacific Press Publishing Association." See also Richard B. Lewis, *Streams of Light: The Story of the Pacific Press* (Mountain View, Calif.: Pacific Press, 1958).
30. McCumber, *Pioneering*, 156, 157; Walter C. Utt, *A Mountain, a Pickax, a College: History of Pacific Union College* (Angwin, Calif.: Alumni Association of Pacific Union College, 1968).
31. The fascinating story of Czechowski is found in Rajmund Ladyslaw Dabrowski and B. B. Beach, eds., *Michael Belina Czechowski, 1818-1876* (Warsaw, Poland: "Znaki Czasu" Publishing House, 1979).
32. Schwarz, *Light Bearers*, 142, 143. For the most comprehensive treatment of Andrews' life and work, see Harry Leonard, ed., *J. N. Andrews: The Man and the Mission* (Berrien Springs, Mich.: Andrews University Press, 1985).
33. B. L. Whitney, "The Central European Mission," in *Historical Sketches of the Foreign Missions of the Seventh-day Adventists* (Basel, Switzerland: Imprimerie Polyglotte, 1886), 16.
34. *Seventh-day Adventist Encyclopedia* (1976 ed.), s.v., "Switzerland."
35. For discussions of the life and work of Conradi, see Gerhard Padderatz, "Conradi und Hamburg: Die Anfänge der deutschen Adventgemeinde," doctoral dissertation, University of Kiel,

1978; Daniel Heinz, *Ludwig Richard Conradi: Missionar der Siebenten-Tags-Adventisten in Europa* (Frankfurt am Main: Peter Lang, 1986); Daniel Heinz, "Ludwig Richard Conradi: Patriarch of European Adventism," *Adventist Heritage* 12 (Winter 1987), 17-24.

36. *Seventh-day Adventist Encyclopedia* (1976 ed.), s.v. "Germany," "Friedensau Predigerseminar," "Erholungsheim Friedensau."

37. *131st Annual Statistical Report—1993* (Silver Spring, Md.: General Conference of Seventh-day Adventists, 1994), 2, 3.

38. See chapters 1, 2, and 4 in this book and Robert S. Folkenberg, "Church Structure—Servant or Master?" *Ministry*, June 1989, 4-9.

Part IV

The Relation of
Institutions and
Lifestyle to Mission

Chapter 7

Mission and Institutional Vitality:

The Dynamics of Educational Expansion

"Concerning church schools," summarized C. C. Lewis in 1888, "it was the unanimous opinion that great care should be exercised in starting out. A poor Seventh-day Adventist school would be about the poorest thing in the world." This statement was part of Lewis's report to the church of the first Adventist teachers' convention. Adventists, he pointed out, were not willing to support Christian schools with either their sympathies or their means.[1] The essence of the Adventist attitude toward Christian education 44 years after the Great Disappointment of 1844 can be captured in two words—*caution* and *apathy*.

To Adventists living in the mid 1990s, it may seem that Christian education has been central to their church from its inception. However, that is far from the truth. Formal education, in fact, was the last major institutional development within the denomination. It was preceded by the establishment of the publishing work in 1849, centralized church organization in 1863, and the health-care program in 1866. By way of contrast, the Adventist church established its first school in 1872 and did not have an extensive elementary system until nearly 1900, despite the fact that as early as 1881 the General Conference had recommended the widespread establishment of schools.[2]

In 1890 the Seventh-day Adventist Church had six elementary

schools, five secondary schools, and two institutions that presumptuously bore the name "college." On the other hand, by 1900 the church could list 220 elementary schools and a worldwide system composed of 25 secondary schools and colleges. That this shift in educational thinking was not a temporary fad is indicated by Figure 3.

The change in Adventist attitudes toward education in the 1890s did not reverse itself. By 1930 the denomination was sponsoring 1,977 elementary schools and 201 higher schools. In 1993 the church had a worldwide system of 4,492 elementary schools, 953 secondary schools, and 85 colleges and universities.

With these facts in mind, we are led to inquire into the reasons for the transformation of the church's educational mentality in the 1890s. Two major answers were developing in the late 1880s.

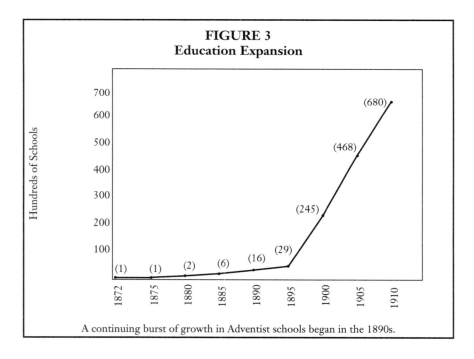

FIGURE 3
Education Expansion

A continuing burst of growth in Adventist schools began in the 1890s.

Spiritual Revival

The first stimulus flowed out of the 1888 General Conference session, with its emphasis on the centrality of salvation through faith in Jesus. Even though the "new" emphasis was largely rejected by the leaders attending the session, it was destined for wide acceptance in the early 1890s due to the teaching and preaching of A. T. Jones, E. J. Waggoner, and Ellen White. These leaders preached and taught in the late 1880s and early 1890s at camp meetings, workers' gatherings, and in local churches across the United States. By the end of the decade Waggoner could tell the 1899 General Conference session that the principles they preached had "been accepted to a considerable extent."[3]

Of greatest importance for the future of Adventist education were the ministerial institutes held during the post-1888 winters, under the direction of W. W. Prescott, leader of the General Conference educational work. These institutes were aimed especially at enlightening the denomination's clergy regarding the centrality of righteousness by faith to Adventism's teaching and mission.[4]

Early in 1891 Prescott decided to provide a similar institute for Adventist educators. This crucial meeting took place at Harbor Springs, Michigan, during July and August 1891. W. C. White described the meetings in terms of spiritual revival, stressing the emphasis on spontaneous personal testimonies. He noted that each day began with A. T. Jones' expositions of the book of Romans. Ellen White also spoke on such topics as the necessity of a personal relationship with Christ, the need for a spiritual revival among the educators attending the convention, and the centrality of the Christian message to education.[5]

Prescott asserted at the 1893 General Conference session that Harbor Springs had marked the turning point in Adventist education. "While the general purpose up to that time," he claimed, "has [sic] been to have a religious element in our schools, yet since that institute, as never before, our work has been *practically* [rather than theoretically] upon that basis, showing itself in courses of study and plans of work as it had not previously."[6]

Before Harbor Springs, the teaching of Bible had held a minor place in Adventist education. However, the convention adopted a recommendation calling for four years of Bible study for students in Adventist colleges. Specifically, the delegates decided that "the Bible as a whole should be studied as the gospel of Christ from first to last; and in which it should be made to appear that all the doctrines held by Seventh-day Adventists were simply the gospel of Christ rightly understood."[7] The convention also recommended the teaching of history from the perspective of the biblical worldview.

The Christocentric revival in the church's theology had led to spiritual revival in its educational program, accompanied by a clearer vision of its purpose. As a direct result, noted Prescott, "during the last two years there has been more growth in the educational work than in the 17 years preceding that time."[8]

Ellen White sailed for Australia three months after the close of the institute. She took with her a heightened awareness of the possibilities of Christian education and of the implications of the gospel for education. While in Australia she would have an unequaled opportunity to influence the development of the Avondale School for Christian Workers along the lines of the principles enunciated at Harbor Springs.

One advantage Mrs. White had in Australia is that she was free from the influence of the conservative Adventist educators in the United States who were having a difficult time deciding to commit themselves wholeheartedly to the Harbor Springs ideal. Thus she was more free to experiment without the hindrance of an established tradition. The Australian school, which emphasized the spiritual and had a service orientation, would develop into a model school under the direction of its reforming founders.[9]

Out of the Avondale experience, which can be viewed as an extension of Harbor Springs, flowed a constant stream of letters and articles on Christian education from the pen of Ellen White. These writings, along with the publication of *Christian Eduction* in 1893 and *Special Testimonies on Education* in 1897, helped guide the development of existing Adventist schools and generated a pervasive awareness among Adventist leaders and members of the importance of Christian education.

Ellen White's counsel on elementary education during the mid-nineties was particularly important to the spread of Adventist education. School attendance was required in Australia. With that situation in mind, she wrote to W. C. White in May 1897: "In this country parents are compelled to send their children to school. Therefore in localities where there is a church, *schools should be established, if there are no more than six children to attend.*"[10]

Counsel such as this was read by reformers in America, including Edward Sutherland and Percy Magan, who immediately began to push for the rapid development of an Adventist elementary system. Years later, Sutherland, who had been converted to the relevance of Ellen White's counsels at Harbor Springs, recalled with some exaggeration that "Magan, Miss DeGraw, and myself [sic] practically at the end of every week would pick up a teacher and go out and establish three schools before Monday morning."[11]

Under the leadership of Sutherland, Magan, and Ellen White before the turn of the century and Frederick Griggs afterward, the Adventist elementary movement continued to accelerate.[12] The writings and personal influence of these leaders moved local congregations to establish an ever-larger number of schools.

The elementary school movement also stimulated expansion in the church's secondary and higher education. This occurred in part because of the increased need for Adventist elementary teachers, but, more importantly, it resulted from the belief that every Adventist young person should have a Christian education.

Minneapolis, with its stress on Christ's righteousness, Harbor Springs, Avondale, and the elementary school movement were not unrelated. Each event led to the next and resulted in vigor and growth throughout the system. On one hand, spiritual revival led to a greater awareness of the need for and potential of Christ-centered education. On the other hand, developing a more distinctively Christian education increased the demand for the product. Between 1888 and 1900 this dynamic process helped transform the Adventist attitude toward church-sponsored schools.

Mission Explosion

A second major stimulus to the expansion of Adventist education in the 1890s was the unprecedented growth of the denomination's mission program. Like the spiritual revival that it paralleled, the mission explosion developed from events of the late 1880s.

It is important to realize from the outset that the mission enthusiasm of the 1890s was not restricted to the Adventist Church. As we saw in chapter 5, the 1890s witnessed unprecedented mission expansion by Americans and Western Europeans as they sought to take the Gospel message to every corner of the earth.

We earlier noted that one of the main stimulants to that expansion was the Student Volunteer Movement for Foreign Missions. Its motto was "The evangelization of the world in this generation." Within a few years of its beginning in 1886, the Student Volunteer Movement had had thousands of young people pledge their lives to mission service.[13]

Thus the 1890s saw the greatest demonstration of missionary interest in American history. American Protestants began to take special concern for such places as India, Africa, Latin America, and the Orient.

The foremost educational result of that mission thrust was the rise of the missionary college and Bible institute movement among American evangelicals. The aim of these schools was to quickly prepare large numbers of workers to staff mission outposts both at home and overseas.

These new schools focused on practical training and Bible knowledge, while avoiding academic degrees and rigorous intellectual training. They did not try to replace regular colleges, but sought to provide "gapmen" who could stand between the ordained minister and the ordinary layman. The first of these schools was established in 1883 as the Missionary Training College for Home and Foreign Missionaries and Evangelists (now called Nyack College).[14]

Events within the Seventh-day Adventist Church paralleled both the mission explosion of evangelical Protestantism and its educational extension. We noted in chapter 5 that signs of new life in Adventist missions began to surface in the mid-1880s. The same year that witnessed the rise of the Student Volunteer Movement also saw the publication of Adventism's first book on foreign missions.

Three years later S. N. Haskell led a two-year fact-finding tour around the world, during which he surveyed the possibilities for opening mission work in various places. Haskell's tour and the publication of *Historical Sketches of the Foreign Missions of the Seventh-day Adventists* did much to promote the missionary spirit among Adventists. By 1890 the stage was set for what Richard Schwarz has called the era of "Mission Advance" in the Adventist denomination.[15]

That advance was fueled by an eschatological excitement that has never been duplicated in Adventist history. Beginning with the Blair Sunday Rest Bill in 1888, the next seven years saw a rash of national Sunday bills and the aggressive persecution of Adventists for Sunday desecration in several states as well as in England, Switzerland, South Africa, and other nations.

Jones, Waggoner, Prescott, and Ellen White tied these developments to righteousness by faith as they preached the three angels' messages of Revelation 14 with new vigor and insight. Roy McGarrell's doctoral research has demonstrated that this important combination of Adventist doctrines empowered the dynamic thrust of Adventist missions throughout the world in the 1890s.[16]

In 1880 Adventists had only eight missions and five evangelistic workers outside the United States. In 1890 they still had only eight missions, even though the number of workers had risen to 56. By 1900, however, the number of missions had risen to 42, and the number of evangelistic mission workers to 481.

The last decade of the 19th century initiated an accelerating trend that remained unabated throughout the first 30 years of the 20th century. By 1930 the church was supporting 8,479 evangelistic workers outside North America, representing 270 missions. This outreach had transformed the very nature of Adventism.[17]

Mission outreach had a direct effect on the expansion of Seventh-day Adventist schooling. The denomination looked to its schools to supply workers for its rapidly expanding worldwide work, just as the evangelical expansion of missions had stimulated the Bible institute and missionary college movement to train large numbers of missionaries in a short period of time.

John Harvey Kellogg, who appears to have been the Adventist in closest touch with evangelical educational ideas, was probably the first to develop a missionary school within the denomination. He established the Sanitarium Training School for Medical Missionaries in 1889, followed by the American Medical Missionary College in 1895.[18]

Meanwhile, in the tradition of the Avondale School for Christian Workers (1894), the training schools stimulated by E. A. Sutherland and Percy Magan and the Adventist missionary colleges (such as Washington Missionary College and Emmanuel Missionary College) soon were dotting the Adventist landscape—all of them similar in method and purpose to the schools spawned by the evangelical mission movement.

Mission expansion affected Adventist educational expansion in at least two identifiable ways. First, it greatly increased the number of schools and students in North America, since most of the denomination's early workers came from the United States. Second, Adventists began to establish schools around the world so that workers could be trained in their home fields. By 1900, therefore, not only had Adventist educational institutions greatly expanded in number, but the system also had been internationalized.

The magnitude of this whole process was compounded by unprecedented institutional development during the 1890s. Besides churches and schools, Adventists developed hospitals, publishing houses, and eventually (to a lesser extent) health food factories in the United States and overseas. Thus the schools were called upon to supply ever larger numbers of institutional workers, in addition to evangelistic workers.

We need to recognize that, from its inception, 19th-century Adventist education was inextricably connected with foreign missions. For example, both the opening of the church's first college and the sending of its first missionary took place in 1874. That was no coincidence. The stated purpose of Battle Creek College was to train for mission service at home and in foreign fields.[19] The first great motivation for Adventist schooling had been rooted in mission. The same was true in the 1890s of the second great thrust of Adventist education.

Thus the spread of Adventist education during the 1890s was directly related to (1) the spiritual/theological revival and (2) an enlarged vision of the church's mission to the world.

It is important to note that these were positive motivators. Negative motivators—such as the need to escape from incipient Darwinism and religious skepticism—played a minor role. *Both then and now, Adventist education at its best stands for something of great importance, rather than representing an escape from the non-Christian world.*

We may conclude that the health of Adventist education depends upon its ability to maintain its spiritual identity and sense of mission. Without these distinctive qualities it loses its reason for being. With them it will continue to be a dynamic force in a world in need of redemptive healing.

---

1. C. C. Lewis, "Report of Teachers' Institute," *Review and Herald*, Sept. 4, 1888, 573.

2. "The General Conference Business Proceedings," *Review and Herald*, Dec. 13, 1881, 376.

3. "General Conference Proceedings," Daily Bulletin of the General Conference, Feb. 27, 1899, 94. For more information on the 1888 meetings, see George R. Knight, *From 1888 to Apostasy: The Case of A. T. Jones* (Hagerstown, Md.: Review and Herald, 1987); George R. Knight, *Angry Saints: Tensions and Possibilities in the Adventist Struggle Over Righteousness by Faith* (Hagerstown, Md.: Review and Herald, 1989).

4. Gilbert M. Valentine, "Controversy: A Stimulus in Theological Education," *Adventist Review*, Nov. 3, 1988, 11, 12. For more on the important contributions of Prescott to SDA education, see Gilbert M. Valentine, *The Shaping of Adventism: The Case of W. W. Prescott* (Berrien Springs, Mich.: Andrews University Press, 1992).

5. W. C. White to E. R. Jones, July 28, 1891; for the most complete treatment of the Harbor Springs convention, see Craig S. Willis, "Harbor Springs Institute of 1891: A Turning Point in Our Educational Conceptions," term paper, Andrews University, 1979.

6. W. W. Prescott, "Report of the Educational Secretary," *Daily Bulletin of the General Conference*, Feb. 23, 1893, 350.

7. Ibid.

8. Ibid., 357.

9. See Milton Hook, "The Avondale School and Adventist Educational Goals, 1894-1900," Ed.D. dissertation, Andrews University, 1978.

10. Ellen G. White to W. C. White, May 5, 1897; cf. Ellen G. White, *Testimonies for the Church* (Mountain View, Calif.: Pacific Press, 1948), 6:198, 199. (Italics supplied.)

11. E. A. Sutherland, "Chapel Talk Before the Medical Students at Los Angeles," December 14, 1949; E. A. Sutherland, tape recording of autobiographical address presented at the College of Medical Evangelists, 1946.

12. For Sutherland's contribution, see Warren Sydney Ashworth, "Edward Alexander Sutherland and Seventh-day Adventist Educational Reform: The Denominational Years, 1890-1904," Ph.D. dissertation, Andrews University, 1986, 141-160. For that of Griggs, see Arnold Collin Reye, "Frederick Griggs: Seventh-day Adventist Educator and Administrator," Ph.D. dissertation, Andrews University, 1984, passim.

13. John R. Mott, "Report of the Executive Committee," in *Student Mission Power: Report of the First International Convention of the Student Volunteer Movement for Foreign Missions, Held at Cleveland, Ohio, U.S.A., February 26, 27, 28 and March 1, 1891* (Pasadena, Calif.: William Carey Library, 1979), 21-23; Ernest R. Sandeen, *The roots of Fundamentalism* (Grand Rapids, Mich.: Baker, 1978), 183; Sydney E. Ahlstrom, *A Religious History of the American People* (New Haven:

Yale University Press, 1972), 864.

14. See Virginia Lieson Brereton, *Training God's Army: The American Bible School, 1880-1940* (Bloomington, Ind.: Indiana University Press, 1990); S. A. Witmer, *The Bible College Story: Education With Dimension* (Manhasset, N.Y.: Channel Press, 1962), 35-37; Sandeen, *Roots of Fundamentalism*, 181-183; George R. Knight, "Early Adventist Education: Attitudes and Context," in George R. Knight, ed., *Early Adventist Educators* (Berrien Springs, Mich.: Andrews University Press, 1983), 7, 8.

15. R. W. Schwarz, *Light Bearers to the Remnant* (Mountain View, Calif.: Pacific Press, 1979), 214.

16. Roy Israel McGarrell, "The Historical Development of Seventh-day Adventist Eschatology, 1884-1895." Ph.D. dissertation, Andrews University, 1989, 277-283.

17. *SDA Encyclopidia*, 1976 ed., s.v. "Missions."

18. See Knight, "Early Adventist Education," 8. For more on Kellogg's educational contributions, see Richard W. Schwarz, "John Harvey Kellogg: Individualist," in Knight, *Early Adventist Educators*, 95-114.

19. See, for example, G. I. Butler, "What Use Shall We Make of Our School?" *Review and Herald*, July 21, 1874, 45.

CHAPTER 8

Mission and Lifestyle:

Amish, Methodists, Adventists and Changing Standards and Values

The Amish are a delightful people. They are a people in desperate earnestness regarding the maintenance of their forebears' church standards—so earnest, in fact, that they are conspicuous for their success. Living in southern Michigan, it is my privilege to visit the Indiana Amish communities from time to time. It is not difficult to be impressed by a people who in all sincerity drive the horse-drawn vehicles and wear the clothes of an age gone by. (On the other hand, I always smile at their young ladies wearing jogging shoes along with their traditional bonnets and ageless dresses. One can only wonder at the odd combination. Perhaps the reason is that they don't have a "quotation" or proof text from their founders on that point.)

The Amish may be the best example of a modern American people who have managed to transfer their church standards across time with very little change. Unfortunately, however, their success has come at the price of their mission to the world. Their very success has cut them off from effective witness. They are viewed by most people as harmless relics; a subculture separated from the world around them by their practice of majoring in the particulars of a previous time and place.[1]

At the other end of the transmission-of-church-standards spectrum is the United Methodist Church. The Methodists once held extremely high church standards that were similar to those of Seventh-day Adventists (a denomination that might be viewed as a niece of the Methodist movement). During the last half of the nineteenth century and the early part of the twentieth, however, Methodism began to relax its position on standards, and by the 1970s it had largely blended into the American culture. One got the impression that to be a Methodist was to be a mainline American—people didn't even need to change their lifestyle to join the church. The result, interestingly enough, was once again a loss of mission.

Dean Kelley, in *Why Conservative Churches Are Growing*, points out that when Methodism's standards became virtually indistinguishable from those of mainline America, its membership began to rapidly decline. Why? Because, claims Kelley (a prominent United Methodist minister and a departmental director in the National Council of Churches), people desire to belong to a church that stands for something, if they are going to join one at all.[2]

Seventh-day Adventists can learn lessons from both the Amish and the Methodists. They need to remember, in contrast to the Methodist experience, that church standards and distinctly Christian values are important. But they also need to learn from the Amish conundrum that standards do change with time and place. The question, of course, is how can churches, schools, parents, and young people come to grips with change in their institutional and personal lives? How does a group or an individual preserve the purpose of the standard or value in the flux of cultural transition?

The present chapter will seek to provide a partial answer to such queries by examining the historical process by which Seventh-day Adventists have developed standards in the past and how they do so in the present. That examination will be followed by a brief discussion of the problems inherent in Adventism's historical practice, and some possible correctives to a process that is not always functional.

Adventism is at present in the midst of a critical juncture in its development. The church has yet to face successfully two facts: (1) modernity and (2) that Adventism has acquired a century and a half of traditions that may or may not be helpful in preparing people to live as Christians in the twenty-first century. One party in Adventism would pull it toward the Amish solution, while another group would allow the church to drift toward the uncritical assimilation of culture.

The burden of this chapter is that the denomination face the challenges of modernity responsibly from a Christian perspective. That will not happen by accident. The present chapter hopes to demonstrate that Adventists can learn not only from the Amish and Methodists, but that they can also learn from their own history as they seek to face the future both responsibly and "Christianly."

Early Adventism and the Formation of Standards

"I once," writes Trinity College's Douglas Frank, "read about certain primitive tribespeople who, when asked how they had come to live in their spot of earth, informed the inquisitive anthropologist that their ancestors had descended from the heavens on a vine." Frank admits that he grew up thinking something quite similar about where evangelicals had come from. They "were simply the current manifestation of the first-century church, and modified very slightly, after a long period of Roman darkness, by the Protestant Reformation."[3]

Frank's confession is quite helpful, because it reflects the approach of many Seventh-day Adventists to standards, values, and church history. It is therefore of the utmost importance at the outset to plainly state that the concerns of mid-nineteenth-century Adventism were those of its culture. Likewise, its solutions were generally the solutions of other conservative American evangelical groups of the time. All were facing the same situation, all were using the Bible to find answers, and it is not especially surprising that they often arrived at similar conclusions regarding values and standards.

As a result, one can learn a great deal about Adventism by studying such groups as the Methodists, Baptists, and (later in the century) the Nazarenes. Their interests were generally those of the early Adventist leaders. All were concerned with issues rooted in a nineteenth-century American culture that was in the process of secularizing. Many of the issues and questions they faced did not present themselves to Paul in the first century or to Luther in the sixteenth. Other issues had been rather constant across the Christian era.

Thus, a first conclusion to note is that early Adventists were children of their time.[4] As children of their time, they lived in a cultural milieu in which such standards as strict Sabbath observance (the Sunday-Sabbath for most Americans),[5] avoidance of worldly entertainment and cheap novels, abstinence from alcoholic beverages, "Puritan" approaches to personal adornment, and so on, were built into the very fabric of conservative American evangelicalism. Most churches had "rules" on such issues, and Adventism was no exception.

Our question is, "How did the early Adventists go about developing their particular approach to forming standards?" The answer varies with the issue.

The Case of Beards and Mustaches

One approach was to respond to a local crisis with church legislation. Thus the Battle Creek Adventist Church passed a series of resolutions on dress on April 30, 1866. The congregation felt constrained to express its views on the subject because "of the present corrupt and corrupting state of the world, and the shameful extremes to which pride and fashion are leading their votaries, and the danger of some among us, especially the young, being contaminated by the influence and example of the world around them." As a result, they passed a series of resolutions which "are truly scriptural . . . and will commend themselves to the Christian taste and judgment of our brethren and sisters everywhere."

Heading the resolutions was one stating that dress should be "SCRU-PULOUSLY PLAIN." Therefore, "we regard plumes, feathers, flowers, and all superfluous bonnet ornaments, as only the *outward* index of a vain heart, and as such are not to be tolerated in any of our members." Also condemned as being antiscriptural were "*every species* of gold, silver, pearl, rubber, and hair [made from hair] jewelry." Beyond that, "a profuseness of ribbons, cording, braid, embroidery, buttons, & c., in dress trimming, are vanities condemned by the Bible." Fancy female hairstyles, of course, fell under the ban.

Surprisingly, however, male shaving habits also were the target of this legislation. Some of the men were trimming their beards by shaving part of their face, while others were "coloring" their beards. In those activities, claimed the resolution, "some of our brethren display a species of vanity equally censurable with that of certain of the sisters in dressing the hair." In every case, they should "discard every style which will betoken the air of the fop." The church had "no objections to a growth of beard on all parts of the face, as nature designed it," yet it was a great error if any portion of the beard was removed. Such "brethren greatly err from the sobriety of the Christian in donning the moustache or goatee." Thus orthodox Adventist males were to be either cleanly shaven or full-bearded; there was to be no fancy work on their faces to encourage vanity.[6]

Such was the standard of the Battle Creek Church. But what were good "Bible standards" for one congregation might be helpful to the entire denomination. Thus on May 17, 1866, the General Conference in session put is imprimatur on the Battle Creek resolutions; thereby providing them with a kind of Adventist *ex cathedra* authority. The session "unanimously adopted" the resolutions.[7]

The Case of Noncombatancy

A second approach to the formation of standards utilized the pages of the *Review and Herald* for hammering out a consensus. A helpful illustration of that tactic is the case of the Adventist approach to the bearing of arms in time of war. The American Civil War (1861-1865) forced the developing denomination to adopt a position.

The debate was initiated by James White's controversial editorial "The Nation," published in August 1862. White felt compelled to make a public statement, because some were questioning the loyalty of Adventists to the Union. He provided evidence for their loyalty, but explained that Adventists had not become active in the conflict because "the fourth precept of the law says, 'Remember the Sabbath day to keep it holy;' the sixth says, 'Thou shalt not kill.' " (It should be noted that at that time noncombatant options did not exist, nor was the compulsory draft in effect.)

Thus the denomination's position on the sacredness and perpetuity of the Ten Commandments had kept its members out of military activity, since its position on God's law was "not in harmony with all the requirements of war." As a result, Adventist young men could not conscientiously volunteer for service.

At that juncture, White set forth the controversial argument that "in the case of drafting, the government assumes the responsibility of the violation of the law of God, and it would be madness to resist. He who would resist until, in the administration of military law, he was shot down, goes too far, we think, in taking the responsibility of suicide." Urging church members to render to Caesar his due, the denomination's president suggested that "those who despise civil law, should at once pack up and be off for some spot on God's foot-stool where there is no civil law."[8]

"The Nation" set off a barrage of correspondence on the topic. Two weeks later, White reported that some of the brethren had reacted "in rather a feverish style." He added that if any of the Adventist draft resisters chose "to have a clinch with Uncle Sam rather than to obey," they could try it. James noted that he had no burden to contend with them, "lest some of you nonresistants get up a little war before you are called upon to fight for your country." Then, significantly, he added that "any well-written articles, calculated to shed light upon our duty as a people in reference to the present war, will receive prompt attention."[9]

That invitation brought forth a flood of articles on the subject from every vantage point. The next four months witnessed the debate publicly carried out through the pages of the denomination's semiofficial paper.

By the end of the war the United States had begun to make provisions for noncombatant service for religiously motivated conscientious objectors, and the Seventh-day Adventist Church had come to somewhat of a consensus on accepting that option as the best one in a less than ideal situation.

The issue, however, was far from settled. As a result, in the postwar years, the General Conference assigned J. N. Andrews the task of developing a comprehensive position paper on the topic.[10] That job, apparently, was never completed, and the denomination would continue to struggle with the issue in the twentieth century. The important point to note at this juncture, however, is that the denomination arrived at a sort of unofficial consensus through the process of airing the varied arguments on the topic through the pages of the *Review*.

The Case of the Beginning of the Sabbath

A third approach to the formation of standards utilized assigned position papers. That procedure was used to settle such issues as financial stewardship and the time to begin the Sabbath.[11]

Despite the fact that the New England Puritans kept their Sabbath (Sunday strictly kept) from sunset to sunset and the Seventh Day Baptists (who introduced the Adventists to the biblical Sabbath) did the same; early Adventists kept their Sabbath from 6:00 p.m. Friday until 6:00 p.m. Saturday. The leader in this departure was the revered Joseph Bates, who had introduced James and Ellen White to the seventh-day Sabbath in 1846. Ex-ship-captain Bates came to this conclusion as a result of his knowledge of the seamen's computation of equatorial time.[12]

Not all, however, were happy with Bates's conclusions on the topic. James White would later recall that some had called the six-o'clock position into question as early as 1847, with "some maintaining that the Sabbath commenced at sun-rise [sic], while others claimed Bible evidence in favor of sunset."[13] The unrest over the question led to an airing of opinions in the *Review*, with progressively more authors favoring the sunset position. Bates replied in March 1851, adding fresh arguments for the six-o'clock time and seeking to demonstrate from Scripture that the Jewish "even" was 6:00 p.m.[14]

Fearing division over the topic in the sparse ranks of the Sabbatarian Adventists, White commissioned J. N. Andrews to devote his time to a study of the topic from the Bible. That study, claimed Andrews, was the denomination's first thorough investigation. Although he had previously held to the six o'clock time, Andrews was soon convinced that "the unanimous testimony of Scriptures is . . . that each day commences with the setting of the sun."[15]

Andrews' well-documented position paper was published in the *Review* of December 4, 1855. About that same time, it was read before a general meeting of Sabbatarian Adventists at Battle Creek. The reading was followed by a discussion. All were convinced on the sunset time, White claimed, except Bates and a few others.[16]

At the close of the 1855 meeting that decided the issue, a special season of prayer was held. In that meeting, White recalled in 1868, "Mrs. W. had a vision, one item of which was that [the] sunset time was correct. This settled the matter with Bro. Bates and others, and general harmony has since prevailed among us upon this point."

That statement compelled James to ask why God hadn't used the visions to put the Adventists straight in the first place. His answer is insightful:

> It does not appear to be the desire of the Lord to teach his people by the gifts of the Spirit on the Bible questions until his servants have diligently searched his word. . . . Let the gifts have their proper place in the church. God has never set them in the very front and commanded us to look to them to lead us in the path of truth and the way to Heaven. His word he has magnified. The Scriptures of the Old and New Testaments are man's lamp to light up his path to the kingdom. Follow that. But if you err from Bible truth, and are in danger of being lost, it may be that God will in the time of his choice correct you, and bring you back to the Bible, and save you.[17]

Thus thoroughly researched position papers were used at times to determine a standard. Such was the case in the disagreement over the time to begin and end the Sabbath. The same procedure would be followed in the area of financial stewardship and other disputed issues.

The Case of Healthful Living

A fourth approach to the formation of Adventist standards was through the urging of Ellen White. That approach would especially be evident in the realm of responsibility for healthful living.

Mrs. White was certainly not the first health reformer among the Sabbatarian Adventists. That role was amply filled by Joseph Bates, who as an unconverted sea captain had given up ardent spirits in the 1820s, when he realized that he looked forward to his daily portion more than he did to his food. A year later he gave up wine. Those abstinences were followed by the forsaking of tobacco, tea, and coffee. By February 1843, in the midst of his Millerite experience, Bates finally gave up flesh foods and richly seasoned dishes.[18]

Bates, although a strict health reformer himself, did not regard health reform as a religious issue of "present truth" to the Advent message. As a result, he remained silent on the topic. According to James White, when Bates was asked why he didn't partake of certain foods, "his usual reply was, 'I have eaten my share of them.' He did not mention his views of proper diet in public at that time, nor in private, unless questioned on the subject."[19] Bates's silence would turn to open advocacy in the early 1860s.

The reason for Bates's shift was apparently Ellen White's vision of June 6, 1863. Before that date, she had written on health from time to time, but it had not been especially prominent in her writings. In fact, in 1858 she had rebuked S. N. Haskell for making abstinence from swine's flesh an issue. Two or three years later, she encouraged a Sister Curtis to feel free in using swine's flesh if her husband desired to eat it. In an act of validation as to where they stood, James penned a note on the back of the Curtis letter with these sentiments: "That you may know how we stand on this question, I would say that we have just put down a two hundred pound porker."[20]

As the Whites saw it up through the early 1860s, health reform was not present truth.[21] Teaching it at that stage could be divisive and schismatic. After all, they were desperately seeking to hold a people together, many of whom believed that the first step toward organization was the first step toward becoming Babylon. The battle for the organization of the Seventh-day Adventist Church was fought between 1859 and 1863. In 1861 the first local conferences were formed. The final victory came on May 21, 1863, when the local conferences banded together in the General Conference of Seventh-day Adventists.

With the organizational battle over, the emphasis on "present truth" broadened two weeks later when Mrs. White had her June 6 vision on health reform. From her perspective, God was leading His people into wholeness step by step. On that very day, she penned a manuscript that indicates a major shift in her thinking. "I saw," she penned, "that it was a sacred duty to attend to our health, and arouse others to their duty." She went on to note that Adventists had a duty to speak out "against intemperance of every kind" and then to point others to God's natural remedies. Adventists were to "wake up minds to the subject" of health.[22]

Thus Ellen White, beginning in June 1863, began to urge higher health standards on Adventists as a matter of religious duty. By December 1865, she had tied healthful living to the central concept of Adventist self-understanding, when she claimed that "health reform . . . is a part of the third angel's message" and is connected to it like "the arm . . . to the human body." Health reform, she pointed out, was one of God's agencies to prepare His people for translation.[23] Through her urging, high standards in healthful living would become an integral part of Seventh-day Adventism.

An Interlocking Mixture of Procedures

We have seen that four major avenues for the formation of church standards in early Adventism were church legislation, the use of the *Review and Herald* to hammer out a consensus, the assignment of biblically based position papers, and the urging of Ellen White. Those methods were not mutually exclusive, nor do they exhaust the field. A perusal of the *Review* suggests that values and standards were "eased" into Adventist lifestyle and tradition by editorials, question-and-answer features, reports from the Battle Creek "Bible Class" that examined thorny issues and publicly reported its conclusions, the publication of articles by Adventist authors and articles selected from other periodicals, and letters published from "stray Adventists" who had a burden on this point or that.

Editorial control, in the form of selection of materials, undoubtedly did much to shape Adventist thinking. It is difficult to overestimate the power of the *Review* as a shaper of Adventism in its early decades. The believers of those times were few in number, were not diverted by the mass media of later times, and generally had no regular preacher. For those folks, the church paper was a major cultural factor in shaping their thoughts and practices.

Also of crucial importance to early Adventist value formation were the articles and personal letters (testimonies) of Ellen White. Her prolific pen over time addressed nearly every contemporary issue related to standards and values on the Adventist horizon. The eventual publication of her most important counsel gave Adventists everywhere a ready resource that they could consult in their day-to-day decision making. Thus her influence in the formation of Adventist values and lifestyle should not be underestimated. That influence undoubtedly grew throughout the nineteenth century as the volume of her counsel multiplied and as Adventists, both individually and collectively, developed the habit of examining the "red books" in their decision making.

An Evaluation of Early Adventism's Approach to the Formation of Values and Standards

There are several things that should be noted about the way early Adventists developed values and standards. First, they were children of their time and place. As a result, they started out as individuals and as a religious group with a very large amount of "cultural baggage" that they had imbibed from their milieu. Their interchange with their culture was an ongoing process. Therefore, we must never forget that their answers to issues of value and standards were related to questions of their time and place and may not always be issues of proportionate importance for those living in the late twentieth century. Thus, while some of their decisions are of permanent value, others may suffer from transitory utility. Some, undoubtedly, are only of value to those who have a historical curiosity (e.g., the ruling on shaving).

Second, Seventh-day Adventist interests in the formation of standards were nearly always related to practical, concrete, and quite specific problems in their daily existence. That is even true of Ellen White's counsels. She wrote her testimonies to meet specific crises; to address concrete issues that were immediately perplexing to her readers.

Third, Adventists had no systematic procedure for the formation of standards. Their approach to doctrinal formulation and dissemination prior to and during the Sabbatarian Conferences of 1848-1850 appears to have been much more systematic than the ad hoc procedures they used to meet issues in lifestyle and standards. Their approach to value formation was even more unconscious.

Fourth, the repeated similarity of their ad hoc answers to meet specific situations gradually grew into a system of Adventist cultural tradition. While Adventists have soundly condemned other churches for relying on their traditions as religious authority, they have yet to come to grips with the reality of the powerful dynamics of 150 years of tradition in their own midst. Denominational traditions take on a life of their own. They may or may not be healthy, biblical, or helpful, but they must all periodically be evaluated rigorously and honestly in the light of Scripture. That truth was central to Jesus' teachings, and it is especially illustrated in the Sermon on the Mount.

Modern Adventism and the Formation of Standards

Having examined nineteenth-century Adventism's approach to the formulation of standards, we now turn to present realities. The most obvious reality is that Seventh-day Adventists in the closing years of the twentieth century have not moved beyond the ad hoc procedures of their forebears in the area of the formation of standards. On the other hand, the nineteenth-century methods are probably less effective today than they were a century ago, because the field of acceptable solutions to any given problem has been progressively narrowed by the growing bulk of Adventist tradition. Many people, unfortunately, equate changing the tradition with destroying the faith of the good old days.

In spite of the difficulties, present-day Adventists are still involved in the formation of values and standards. We will briefly examine some of the methods used in that endeavor.

Grab a Quote

The most popular way to argue for (or against) any standard in Adventism is undoubtedly the amassing of Ellen White quotations on the topic. While that procedure is often helpful, it should be done with some wisdom if it is to result in valid conclusions.

Some Adventist quotation grabbers end up with some interesting results that leave much to be desired in terms of Christian principles. Let me illustrate. I once knew a physician (a head elder) who "incessantly ranted" about people being admitted into church membership while wearing a gold wedding band. Yet that same gentleman, with a clear conscience, drove a gold-colored Cadillac. His mentality isn't too hard to unpack. The plain fact is that he had a quotation from Ellen White on gold wedding bands, but had undoubtedly searched her writings in vain for any condemnation of gold Cadillacs. The conclusion was obvious: God forbade the wearing of gold bands but did not frown on the possession of gold Cadillacs.

At this juncture I am not arguing as to whether gold wedding bands (or Cadillacs) are good or bad. My interest is one of relative values, since two Ellen White arguments against wedding bands were based on their cost and irresponsible accommodation to culture.[24] An uninitiated observer (i.e., non-Adventist) might conclude that our physician friend had come perilously close to having swallowed the camel after having carefully strained out the gnat. On the other hand, those of us on the inside know that he was well within the bounds of time-honored Adventist tradition and fully in harmony with the traditionally accepted standards of Adventist mentality.

Since the use and misuse of Ellen White's writings typically stand at the center of Adventist approaches to the formulation of standards, an improved understanding of how to correctly use and interpret her writings (and those of the Bible) is crucial to a healthier approach.[25] We will briefly return to that topic in our final conclusions.

Tradition

A second contemporary force in the realm of Adventist formation and maintenance of standards is tradition. Like other methods, tradition has both positive and negative aspects. On the positive side, tradition means continuity with the past. In other words, we don't have to reinvent a set of Adventist standards every morning; we have the security of belonging to a church with a high set of standards and values that are generally quite beneficial. Ideally, new standards are added in such a way as to harmonize with existing Adventist tradition.

Unfortunately, the very presence of a body of tradition can lead to some interesting practices that are frightfully like some of the Pharisaic dilemmas of old. The ancient Pharisees, for example, ruled that it was unlawful to carry a handkerchief on the Sabbath day because it was work. Of course, if the same item was pinned to one's garment, it was permissible to carry it, since the handkerchief had technically become a part of the garment and no Pharisees were arguing that the wearing of clothes on Sabbath was work. In a similar vein, they had a prohibition against carrying a rock above a certain size on the Sabbath. But on the other hand, it was lawful to carry a child who happened to be carrying the rock, since carrying the child was an act of mercy.

To outside observers it may appear that Adventists have backed themselves into a corner similar to that of the Pharisees on the "rock" issue. After all, it is a hallowed Adventist tradition that it is lawful to carry a "rock" pinned to one's garment, but some sort of sin if the same "rock" is on a string around a person's neck. Of course, in Adventist casuistry it is lawful to wear the aforementioned "rock" suspended from the neck if, and only if, it has a practical use and is no longer a mere ornament. Thus if a clock is implanted in the "rock," it is technically transformed into a marginally useful watch and the problem is solved.

Or what about those "health reformers" who wouldn't eat a piece of meat for any reason but couldn't jog around the block if their lives depended on it? Or how are we to handle the widespread confusion that has become established in Adventism between a healthful diet that ideally aims at getting back to natural foods and the massive Adventist support of food processes that develop meat substitutes that isolate protein and utilize high levels of salt to improve the taste? It seems that many have confused meat substitutes with vegetarianism and vegetarianism with health reform. The inventor of the so-called health foods claimed that he rarely ate them. "I live upon bread, potatoes, and fruits," J. H. Kellogg told a questioner. "I don't eat health foods." He saw them as a bridge from a meat to a vegetarian diet. "If you can't carry out the health reform without a food factory the thing is moonshine." Kellogg had avoided the general Adventist confusion between ends and means in diet.[26]

While tradition is useful as a stabilizing force, mindless tradition is counterproductive. Meaningful tradition must be consciously related to Christian purpose.

Ad Hoc Legislation

A third contemporary approach to the formation of standards is ad hoc decision making both by individuals and local church bodies. These decisions are often closely related to healthy and unhealthy understandings of Ellen White and Adventist tradition. Thus the validity of ad hoc decisions is tied to issues related to those sources of authority.

All too often, however, the offhand decisions of individuals and boards under pressure lead to strange rulings that are difficult for both young people and adults to understand. I remember my first day as a mid-year appointee to the principalship of a metropolitan junior academy. It was during the era of the miniskirt, and one of my first callers was an irate mother who hoped that the school would now have some strict standards. It soon came out that her fifteen-year-old daughter wore her skirts too short. The mother expected me to do something about it. Her suggestion was that the school should have a rule that skirts should be no shorter than two inches above the knee. In my mind, as she talked, I envisioned myself running around with my ruler grabbing young ladies by their knees.

Then, as I listened to this mother expound upon a rule that had been legislated in several academies, my mind drifted onto the outworking of the suggestion. After all, two inches above the knee was mighty long for a girl who stood at 5 feet 11 inches. On the other hand, it would be halfway to the waist for a chubby ninth-grader in my school who was 4 feet 9 inches. If she happened to bend over in such an outfit, nothing would be left to the imagination. During the next week, I called my teachers together. We rejected the suggested rule and adopted a set of principles based on neatness, cleanliness, and modesty; being quite explicit that what was modest for one person might be quite immodest for another. There would be no rule, but every student would be held responsible for meeting the standards reflected in the principles. In this case, we opted against hasty legislation.

On another occasion, I served as the vice-chairman of a school board that had legislated the quite common rule against the wearing of blue and black jeans. Since there were some hard feelings and serious questions over the regulation, I began to ask the board whether the wrongness was in the color or in the material. After all, the students could wear any other color of jeans. Likewise, they could wear black or blue pants made out of any other material. Perhaps, I surmised, there was some kind of metaphysical "sinfulness" in the combining of blue or black with a specific type of material (i.e., jean denim). In the end, the board decided to nullify the rule.

That, it seems to me, was the wise move, since we had some truly important standards to enforce and should not be wasting our time and credibility on rules that didn't make much difference to the quality of student life and development. Too many schools seem to legislate "standards" whose only purpose appears to be to test the tolerance and patience of fairly intelligent young people. There are plenty of meaningful issues without creating such artificial tests of obedience. Both church bodies and individuals need to consider carefully all such legislation in the light of the goals of Christian education. Are we seeking to create pathways or roadblocks to the kingdom through our ad hoc legislation?[27]

Public Exposure of an Issue

At the denominational level, the church's major publications still provide an important avenue for shaping the development of standards and values. James White used this avenue in the early days of the church and it finds significant use today.

I think of it in the framework of the process of capturing an enemy island in World War II. First, the battleships and airplanes would blast and bomb the island day and night for a week or two. Then came the frontal assault by troops in landing crafts.

An Adventist parallel took place in the late 1960s when there was a felt need on the part of some institutions and General Conference departments to modify the denomination's position on accepting government aid. The siege guns of such journals as the *Review* and *Ministry* opened up on the topic from all viewpoints, as the Adventist public became aware of the fact that there were several perspectives. Thus minds were prepared for a possible shift in policy. Then came the frontal assault at the Annual Council in Mexico City in 1972. That meeting resulted in a new set of denominational standards on the issue.[28]

That procedure is a periodic experience in Adventism. One of the most recent topics to receive such exposure has been women's ordination.

Legislation at the General Conference Level

Closely related to the public airing of views through the Adventist media is action by the General Conference at its quinquennial sessions and annual councils. General Conference legislation in relation to standards, of course, is much less off-the-cuff than local decisions. Study commissions, position papers, and documentary source collections from the General Conference Archives and the Ellen G. White Estate generally undergird the recommendations presented to an official conclave. Such systematic procedures have recently been utilized in such areas as Sabbath observance and the use of the tithe.[29]

Summary and Evaluation of Present Approaches to the Formation of Standards

We have seen that present-day Adventists approach value and standard formation largely through the writings of Ellen White, tradition, local rule-making legislation, discussion in church periodicals, and General Conference legislation. These methods, it should be noted, offer no advance over the procedures of the Adventist pioneers. And in many ways a lack of progress in procedures may actually mean a substantial regression in creative ability, since, as we noted earlier, the freedom to navigate among the available options has been hampered by a significant body of "unquestionable" tradition that may or may not be valid from the perspective of biblical Christianity.

A further point of concern is that the denomination has no systematic means for either reviewing past standards or developing standards that face the issues of modern culture. Our individual and collective responses to issues of value and standards are still ad hoc. Instead of consciously crafting a biblically viable set of standards and values, Adventists and their church generally merely react to current crises and problems that force a decision. That, of course, was also the pattern of the denomination in its early years.

One result is that the denomination too often is fighting a rearguard action against the erosion of its standards. Many Adventists are still seeking to convince young people that they should not attend movies because they will meet the wrong kind of people there. Meanwhile, the church and its members stand almost speechless before the VCR and television. We have taught abstinence rather than responsibility in many areas, and now both members and leaders seem to be paralyzed by indecision on issues for which they lack an authoritative quotation, proof text, or traditional denominational stand.

Now such a predicament may be "tolerable" to those of us adults who have dedicated our lives to Adventist Christianity, but it is leaving increasingly larger numbers of Adventist young people cold. An observer gets the impression that more and more of them are taking Adventism and its lifestyle less seriously than previous generations. Many drift out of the church, and a large portion of those who remain do so for cultural, rather than religious, reasons. They are confused by a system that has failed adequately to distinguish between basic Christian doctrines and boundary-marker lifestyle standards, by schools and churches that seemingly have equated going to a movie with rejecting Jesus, and by traditions that have drawn strange lines for some standards that fail to make sense to them.

A few years ago I presented some of these issues to a group of conservative church administrators. I thought I might be putting my job on the line by even raising the problem. To the contrary (and to my relief), I found them very responsive.

They knew the problems as well as I did, but they raised their own challenge to me. They knew what was happening to their young people and that the problems will have to be faced more responsibly in the future if we are to retain the brightest Adventist youth. But, they claimed, if we seek to make biblical sense out of the old lines, approaches, and standards, it will upset those older folks who still identify Christianity and Adventism with the exact positions they were taught in their own youth. To complicate things, the older members are current tithe payers, while most of the young are not yet major contributors.

How, my administrative friends inferred, can we afford to think responsibly in such an atmosphere? That is a very real question. Of course, for the future of the church, the alternate question is just as crucial: How can we afford not to think responsibly?

Thus Adventism, like the ancient Jews and the Christians of the early church and Reformation, has come full circle. From a people fighting against the bonds of tradition, it has become entangled in its own tradition, with no satisfactory way to resolve many of the serious difficulties that face it.

Conclusions

Jürgen Moltmann penned in *The Crucified God* that "for Christian faith to bring about its own decay by withdrawal into the ghetto without self-criticism, is a parallel to its decay through uncritical assimilation."[30]

I am still concerned with the Amish. Through their inability to distinguish between universal Christian principles and the particulars of time and place, they have sought to transfer the world of the sixteenth century into the twentieth. The result has been "ghettoization" and a "decay" of mission. Surely they have been successful, but surely they have failed.

I am still concerned with the mainline Methodists. Through their failure to distinguish between universal Christian principles and the particulars of time and place, they have seemingly "cast out the baby with the bath water." They have taken, in Moltmann's words, the route of "uncritical assimilation." As a result, they have lost their identity as standing for something distinctively Christian and apart from culture. That identity crisis has resulted in "decay" in their mission. Surely they have succeeded, but surely they have failed.

I am still concerned with Adventism, because it faces both temptations: "Ghettoization" on the one hand and "uncritical assimilation" on the other. One sector of the church would pull it one direction, and another wing would pull it the other.

The great temptation for Adventism will be to shut its eyes and hope the problems will go away. But such a course is suicidal. In the long run, ignoring the problems and challenges will lead to an ignoring of the standards themselves. The church (and its members) must face the problems seriously and strenuously if it expects the coming generations to take its time-honored standards seriously. We cannot have one without the other.

Perhaps one of the greatest needs of individual Adventists in this process is to develop the ability to read the Bible and Ellen White's writings more responsibly. Quotation collecting is not enough if we are to make sense out of our standards. People need to learn to read with understanding; an understanding that takes literary and historical contexts into account; an understanding that is able to distinguish between universal principles and the particulars of time and place; an understanding that can apply those universal principles in the 1990s.[31]

One of the most important priorities of corporate Adventism today may be the development of mechanisms to deal with its crisis in values and standards. Such mechanisms should have at least two components: (1) a process for systematic review and (2) an ongoing process for consistent value and standard formation.

The call is not for lower standards, but for higher standards—standards that make sense out of both gold wedding bands and gold Cadillacs; standards that preserve the best of the old, while utilizing the most helpful of the new. Jesus provided a model for the revitalization of standards in the Sermon on the Mount (see Matthew 5:21-48).

Beyond the biblical base, one criterion for every standard and value is its effectiveness in enabling people to internalize Christian principles and the loving character of Christ. Standards and values are not ends in themselves, but means to an end. Every standard and value must be evaluated in the light of the Cross, rather than in the light of Adventist tradition. Such a procedure, it should be noted, will not lead to identity with the surrounding culture, but to a "radical discontinuity" from a culture that is viewed, from the perspective of the cross, as both fallen and in need of redemption.[32]

Another factor to consider in value and standard formation is the mission of the church. The successful accomplishment of Adventism's mission is directly related to a healthy approach to standards and values. People everywhere are hungry for meaning. They are looking for a way of life that makes sense in a world that too often does not. One function of the church is consciously to develop a worldview and a way of life that offers a distinctively Christian alternative to the values, standards, and lifestyles that inundate individuals in their daily existence. Such standards, if they are to forward the mission of the church, must be built upon biblical principles. After all, the church is not to reflect culture, but to help people live as Christians within culture. On the other hand, and at the same time, the church must relate its standards and values to the cultural context in which it finds itself (rather than to some other context) if it is to provide a "meaningful" alternative in its mission to the world.

A major challenge for Adventism in the last decade of the twentieth century is to navigate safely between the perils of "ghettoization" and "uncritical assimilation"; between the pitfalls that have so deeply affected the mission of the Amish and the United Methodists. One of the great lessons of history is that such a course will not be navigated by accident.

---

1. For a fascinating and insightful study of Amish standards and values, see Donald B. Kraybill, *The Riddle of Amish Culture* (Baltimore: Johns Hopkins University Press, 1989).
2. Dean M. Kelley, *Why Conservative Churches Are Growing: A Study in Sociology of Religion* (New York: Harper & Row, 1972), passim.
3. Douglas Frank, *Less Than Conquerors: How Evangelicals Entered the Twentieth Century* (Grand Rapids, Mich.: Eerdmans, 1986), vii.
4. For helpful contextual studies on the world of early Adventism, see Ronald G. Walters, *American Reformers: 1815-1868* (New York: Hill and Wang, 1978); Gary Land, ed., *The World of Ellen G. White* (Washington, D.C.: Review and Herald, 1987); James C. Whorton, *Crusaders for Fitness: The History of American Health Reformers* (Princeton, N.J.: Princeton University Press, 1982); George R. Knight, "Oberlin College and Adventist Educational Reforms," *Adventist Heritage* 8 (Spring 1983):3-9. For a pictoral treatment of nineteenth-century culture, see Otto L. Bettmann, *The Good Old Days—They Were Terrible* (New York: Random House, 1974).
5. See Winton U. Solberg, *Redeem the Time: The Puritan Sabbath in Early America* (Cambridge, Mass.: Harvard University Press, 1977), for the background and mental attitude of Americans toward Sabbath keeping. For a nineteenth-century treatment, see Wilbur F. Crafts, *The Sabbath for Man* (New York: Funk & Wagnalls, 1885).
6. "Resolution on Dress," *Review and Herald*, May 8, 1866, 180.
7. John Byington and Uriah Smith, "Fourth Annual Session of General Conference," *Review and Herald*, May 22, 1866, 196.
8. James White, "The Nation," *Review and Herald*, August 12, 1862, 84. Cf. Ellen G. White, *Testimonies for the Church* (Mountain View, Calif.: Pacific Press, 1948), 1:356.
9. James White, "The Nation," *Review and Herald*, August 26, 1862, 100.
10. J. N. Andrews to George I. Butler, Nov. 24, 1868.
11. Helpful historical treatments of these topics are found in Carl Coffman, "The Practice of Beginning the Sabbath in America," *Andrews University Seminary Studies* 3 (January 1965):9-17; Brian E. Strayer, "Adventist Tithepaying: The Untold Story," *Spectrum* 17 (October 1986):39-52.
12. Joseph Bates, *The Seventh Day Sabbath: A Perpetual Sign* (New Bedford, Mass.: Benjamin Lindsey, 1846), 32.
13. James White, "Time to Commence the Sabbath," *Review and Herald*, Feb. 25, 1868, 168.
14. Joseph Bates, "Time of the Holy Sabbath," *Review and Herald*, April 21, 1851, 71, 72.
15. James White, "Time to Commence the Sabbath," *Review and Herald*, Dec. 4, 1855, 78; J. N. Andrews, "Time for Commencing the Sabbath," Review and Herald, Dec. 4, 1855, 76-78.
16. James White, "Time to Commence the Sabbath," *Review and Herald*, Feb. 25, 1868, 168.
17. Ibid.
18. Joseph Bates, *The Autobiography of Elder Joseph Bates* (Battle Creek, Mich.: Seventh-day Adventist Publishing Assn., 1868), passim; Dores Eugene Robinson, *The Story of Our Health Message* (Nashville, Tenn.: Southern Publishing Assn., 1955), 50-59.
19. E. G. White and James White, *Christian Temperance and Bible Hygiene* (Battle Creek, Mich.: Good Health Pub. Co., 1890), 252.
20. E. G. White, *Testimonies for the Church*, 1:206, 207; J. N. Loughborough, "Sketches of the Past—No. 110," *Pacific Union Recorder* (January 26, 1911), 1; H. E. Carver, *Mrs. E. G. White's Claims to Divine Inspiration Examined* (Marion, Ia.: Advent and Sabbath Advocate Press, 1877), 19, 20; Staff of the Ellen G. White Estate, *A Critique of the Book: Prophetess of Health* (Washington, D.C.: The Ellen G. White Estate, 1976), 45.
21. For a discussion of change in SDA doctrine and lifestyle and the nature of "Present Truth," see

George R. Knight, "Adventists and Change," *Ministry*, October 1993, 10-15.

22. Ellen G. White, "Testimony Regarding James and Ellen White," unpublished manuscript, [June 6], 1863.

23. E. G. White, *Testimonies for the Church*, 1:486.

24. Ellen G. White, *Testimonies to Ministers and Gospel Workers* (Mountain View, Calif.: Pacific Press, 1923), 180, 181.

25. For a discussion of the misuse and proper use of E. G. White's counsel, see George R. Knight, *Myths in Adventism: An Interpretive Study of Ellen White, Education, and Related Issues* (Washington, D.C.: Review and Herald, 1985).

26. "Interview at Dr. J. H. Kellogg's Home, October 7, 1907, between Geo. W. Amadon, Eld. A. C. Bourdeau, and Dr. J. H. Kellogg," unpublished manuscript, 64.

27. See Knight, *Myths in Adventism*, 201-204 for a discussion of effective rules as they relate to principles.

28. Eric Syme, *A History of SDA Church-State Relations in the United States* (Mountain View, Calif.: Pacific Press, 1973), 141-143; "Recommendations of General Interest from the Autumn Council 1972—Part 3," *Review and Herald*, Dec. 14, 1972, 26, 27.

29. "Report of the Ad Hoc Committee on Sabbath Observance," in *1984 Annual Council of the General Conference Committee: General Actions*, 44-56; "Use of Tithe—Guidelines," and "Administration of Tithe Funds—Position Statement," in *1985 Annual Council of the General Conference Committee: General Actions*, 52-54, 79, 80.

30. Jürgen Moltmann, *The Crucified God: The Cross of Christ as the Foundation and Criticism of Christian Theology* (New York: Harper & Row, 1974), 21.

31. See my *Myths in Adventism*, 17-25, for a preliminary treatment of the methodology suggested here. I have treated the problem of quotation collecting in *From 1888 to Apostasy: The Case of A. T. Jones* (Washington, D.C.: Review and Herald, 1987), 230-239.

32. George R. Knight, *Philosophy and Education: An Introduction in Christian Perspective*, 2d. ed. (Berrien Springs, Mich.: Andrews University Press, 1989), 169, 170.

Part V

Adventist Futures in Relation to Adventist Pasts

Chapter 9

The Mainspring of SDA Mission:

Another Look at Adventism's Prophetic Roots

The year 1994 marks the 150th anniversary of the October 22 disappointment of Millerite Adventism. Up to that date the Millerites had been certain that Christ would return in 1844. But suddenly their hopes were shattered; their certainties replaced by disorientation. On October 23 the disappointed Millerites found themselves in the midst of a sudden and unexpected identity crisis.

The Adventist Denominations

The subsequent months and years found those who remained faithful to their advent hope in a search for identity. Who were they? What did it mean to be an Adventist?

The answer to these questions was not obvious at the time. Further Bible study and heart searching were in order. Between 1844 and 1848 three major strands of post-Millerite Adventism evolved.[1] The first was the Spiritualizers. This group gave up the literal interpretation of Scripture and spiritualized the meaning of even concrete words. Thus they could claim that Christ had come on October 22—He had come into their hearts. That was the second coming. This group spawned a large amount of fanaticism.

The second group was the Albany Adventists, so called because they organized along congregational lines at Albany, New York, in May 1845. Their aim was to distance themselves from the fanatics among the Spiritualizers. They continued to look for the cleansing of the sanctuary as the second coming of Christ. Further time-setting sprang up periodically in their midst. The group's proponents eventually gave up any firm belief in Miller's prophetic scheme. Joshua V. Himes and Josiah Litch (Miller's chief lieutenants) belonged to this segment of Adventism, as did William Miller himself up to his death in 1849.

A third group eventually concluded that the Millerites had been correct in the dating of the 2300 days of Daniel 8:14 and that something of importance had happened on October 22, 1844, but the event was not the second advent. Rather it was the beginning of the cleansing of the heavenly sanctuary. This group developed around several key doctrines, including a continuing belief in the near advent of Jesus in the clouds of heaven, the sanctity of the seventh-day Sabbath, Christ's two-apartment ministry in the heavenly sanctuary, the conditional nature of immortality, and the perpetuity of spiritual gifts (including the gift of prophecy).

These Sabbatarian Adventists came to see themselves as the only true heir of pre-Disappointment Adventism, since (unlike the Spiritualizers) its advocates continued to hold to a literal Advent and (unlike the Albany Adventists) they continued to hold to Miller's principles of prophetic interpretation. The foremost leaders of the Sabbatarians were Joseph Bates and James and Ellen White.

Between 1844 and 1866, six denominations arose out of the three branches of Millerism. The Albany Adventists gave birth to four of those denominations—the American Evangelical Conference in 1858, the Advent Christians in 1860, the Church of God (Oregon, Illinois) in the 1850s, and the Life and Advent Union in 1863. The Sabbatarian movement resulted in two denominations, the Seventh-day Adventists between 1861 and 1863 and the Church of God (Seventh Day) in 1866. With their diversity, individuality, and lack of organization, the Spiritualizer wing of Adventism formed no permanent bodies. Various Spiritualizers eventually gravitated to other "isms," more stable Adventist groups, or were absorbed back into the larger culture.

The Changing Shape of Adventism

While membership statistics are not available, it seems safe to suggest that the Evangelical Adventists and the Advent Christians were the most numerous in the early 1860s, with the Advent Christians constantly gaining over the Evangelicals. One reason for the Advent Christians' relatively greater success seems to be that they had unique doctrines that gave them something to stand for. Their doctrines of conditionalism and annihilationism (having to do, respectively, with the unconscious state of humans in death and the final destruction of the wicked) provided a focal point for their identity. Those teachings gradually even surpassed their emphasis on the advent. They became their distinctive doctrines and provided the Advent Christians with a rallying point.

The Evangelicals, on the other hand, had only the premillennial advent to separate them from the general Christian populace. When a significant portion of conservative Protestantism also adopted forms of premillennialism in the decades after the Civil War, Evangelical Adventism had little reason to continue a separate existence. By the early twentieth century it had ceased to exist as a separate religious body.[2]

Statistics among the Adventist groups were not easy to come by in their early years. Some feared that "numbering Israel" might bring a "curse." Others proved to be more helpful, even though reluctant. The divisions and mutual suspicions among the Adventist groups didn't make the task any easier.[3]

The first Adventist census was published by D. T. Taylor in 1860. Taylor counted 584 ministers, with 365 believing in conditionalism and annihilationism, 67 believing in consciousness after death, nine undecided, and 143 not reporting. On the day of worship, 365 held to Sunday, 57 to the seventh day, with 162 not reporting. Taylor estimated 54,000 lay members, but did not attempt to break them down according to belief. However, other sources indicate that somewhat more than 3,000 were Sabbatarians. Thus by 1860 the seventh-day keepers represented a little more than 10 percent of the Adventists. The balance of them, presumably, were first-day worshipers.[4]

Taylor's census also gathered estimates regarding the subscription lists of the various Adventist journals. The Advent Christian *World's Crisis* led the list with 2,900 subscribers. The *Crisis* was followed by the Sabbatarian's *Review and Herald* (2,300) and the Evangelical's *Advent Herald* (2,100). Taylor went out of his way to note that the promoters of the *Review and Herald*, "though a distinct minority, are very devoted, zealous, and active in the promulgation of their peculiar views of the Sunday and Sabbath."[5] The results of that zeal would show up in the decades to come.

The 1890 United States government census not only provides a more accurate picture of Adventist membership but also indicates radical shifts in the relative size of the various Adventist denominations. By that time the Seventh-day Adventists had achieved predominance, with 28,991 members in the United States. The Advent Christians were next, with 25,816. Then came the Church of God (Oregon, Illinois), with 2,872; the Evangelicals, with 1,147; the Life and Advent Union, with 1,018; and the Church of God (Seventh Day), with 647.[6]

A century later only four of the six Adventist denominations still existed. In 1990 the Seventh-day Adventists reported 717,446 members in the United States, while the Advent Christians claimed 27,590, the Church of God (Oregon, Illinois) 5,688, and the Church of God (Seventh-Day) 5,749.[7]

As noted above, the once-strong Evangelical Adventist denomination had been the first to go. It had disappeared in the early twentieth century. The Life and Advent Union had been the next to lose its separate identity. By 1958 the Union reported only 340 members. Six years later it merged with the Advent Christians.[8]

Thus by the early 1990s the Seventh-day Adventists, with their more than 700,000 members in the United States and nearly 8,000,000 members worldwide dominated the ranks of the religious bodies tracing their heritage back to Millerism. As Clyde Hewitt, an Advent Christian historian, put it, "the tiniest of the Millerite offshoot groups was the one which would become by far the largest."[9]

The "Why" of Success

At this point one is left with the question of why? Why did the minute Sabbatarian movement with its unpopular doctrines not only survive but prosper? One can only speculate regarding the answer to that question, but several respectable hypotheses can be argued from the historical data. Before exploring those hypotheses, it should be noted that closely connected to the query as to why Seventh-day Adventism succeeded is a second issue, that of why Millerism succeeded. I suggest that the two movements experienced success for largely the same reasons.

Before moving to my analysis, we should look at the answers that others have supplied to the why of Millerite success. Three helpful answers come from David L. Rowe, Michael Barkun, and Ruth Alden Doan—all non-Adventist scholars who have done extensive study in Millerism.

Rowe points out that while many "prophets" predicting the end of the world have arisen in American history, none achieved a mass following like Miller's. Rowe then goes on to explain the movement's success in terms of revivalism, millennialism, and pietism. All three of those forces met at the time of the Millerite movement. Rowe argues that while Second Awakening revivalism provided the method for spreading Millerism, millennialism supplied the idea or dream of the future kingdom that gave direction to the movement, and pietism furnished the temperament of faith that enabled individuals to respond to the revival and accept the vision of the new world to come. The three working together developed a dynamic that thrust Millerism forward.[10]

Barkun calls attention to environmental factors as contributors to the success not only of Millerism but also of other millennarian and utopian movements of the same era. Thus natural disasters (such as changing weather patterns) and economic/social crises (such as the panic of 1837) provided a climate in which people were looking for solutions to their individual and collective stress. In such a context, Miller's message supplied hope in a world in which human effort had failed to achieve the expected results. There seems to be a rule that the worse things get in human terms, the more feasible millennial options appear to be.[11]

In support of Barkun's point, it is an established fact that millennial groups prosper in times of crisis. Thus Seventh-day Adventist and dispensational evangelism had some of its most successful years during World War I. Likewise, Barkun notes that millennarian revivals took place not only during the economic depression of the 1840s, but also during those of the 1890s and 1930s.[12]

Doan views one factor in the success of Millerism to be its ortho-doxy—its essential harmony with the other religious forces of the day in terms of doctrine, lay leadership in understanding the Bible, and so on. Millerism's one essential heresy was its view of the premillennial advent. But the movement's very orthodoxy in most matters left the populace open to its one unorthodox message. Doan's position, which is currently shared by most non-Adventist scholars, is a reversal from earlier views that treated Millerism as something strange (if not weird) and out of harmony with its culture.[13]

It should be noted that the various suggestions for Millerism's success presented thus far are not mutually exclusive. Each appears to supply a portion of the explanation underlying Millerism's success (and, by extension, the success of Sabbatarian Adventists). But even collectively they supply but a part of the answer to our question.

The suggestions put forth in the rest of this chapter should not be seen as being out of harmony with those set forth by Rowe, Barkun,

Doan, and others, but as being complementary to them. But whereas their suggestions tended to focus on factors external to the Millerite movement, those developed in the rest of this chapter look more carefully at the internal factors that led to the success of pre-1845 Millerism and post-1844 Sabbatarian Adventism. Social forces and contextual factors are important (probably even essential) to the success of any religious movement, but they are not enough by themselves. The external factors are not the movement, but the soil for the successful planting and development of a movement. Both the external and internal factors must be in place for a movement such as Millerism or Sabbatarian Adventism to succeed.

We will now look at four internal factors that seem to have contributed to the success of Millerism and Seventh-day Adventism.

A View of Truth

First, it should be noted that apocalyptic movements often attract two personality types. On one side we find the rationalism that unpacks the biblical prophecies and develops the apocalyptic scheme of events. On the other side are the emotional types that gravitate toward the excitement of the apocalyptic expectancy and often run into fanatical, irrational extremism.

Millerism had both types. Thus although it was founded upon the cool rationalism of Miller, it also had its Starkweathers (a fanatical leader in the pre-Disappointment period), Gorgases (R. C. Gorgas was mixed up in fanaticism on October 22, 1844),[14] and Spiritualizers. A movement disintegrates whenever the rational forces are not strong enough to stem the centrifugal forces of irrationalism or emotionalism. It was in this area that the Spiritualizer wing of Adventism came to nothing. Its irrationalism overcame its rationalism until at last there were no controls on its belief structure.

One of the strengths of Millerism was its rational development of its central doctrine. That element drew believers to its cause through its very logic. But Millerism at its best also made room for religious emotionalism, and that emotionalism ideally took place within the bounds of rationality. That combination gave both life and stability to the movement and heightened its appeal.

Seventh-day Adventism has partaken of much that same balance, although it appears at times to wander too far toward the purely rational pole. Both Millerism and its Sabbatarian offspring, of course, have had their excitable and fanatical elements, but the stability of their success can largely be attributed to their ability to appeal to the rational element in people. Thus they have aimed at converting people to "the truth."

The Content of Truth

A second element that appears to have led to the evangelistic success of Millerism and Seventh-day Adventists is the content or doctrinal factor in their view of truth. Thus Millerism had what it considered to be an important Bible truth to offer to individuals searching for meaning. For Millerism, that doctrinal factor was the premillennial return of Christ. Millerism was not just a part of the ecclesiastical woodwork; it stood for something distinctive from other religious groups. Thus it had a message to preach. Many responded to that message.

As noted above, one of the reasons that Evangelical Adventism died out was that it had lost its doctrinal distinctiveness once a significant portion of American Protestantism accepted premillennialism. After that, Evangelical Adventism had no further reason to exist. As a result, it blended back into generic evangelicalism. On the other hand, the Advent Christians adopted conditionalism as their new doctrinal distinctive. Thus they had at least one more reason to continue a separate existence than their Evangelical sibling.

By way of contrast, the Seventh-day Adventists developed a whole arena of unconventional beliefs that they saw as their special mission to share with the world. Just as a kite flies against the wind, so there is a dynamic in religious movements that is vitalized by differences and even opposition. Being different gives individuals and social groups meaning. And being different develops commitment to a cause, especially when it entails bridge-burning as one joins a religious subculture.[15]

In Millerism that bridge-burning dynamic took place when people were "cast out of Babylon" for espousing premillennial beliefs. An example of that dynamic in Seventh-day Adventism takes place in family and work struggles that involve the keeping of the seventh-day Sabbath in a culture that sees Saturday as a workday.

Seventh-day Adventists have established several doctrinal and lifestyle boundary markers that have had that effect. Hewitt, in seeking to explain Seventh-day Adventist growth in contrast to the lack of growth in his Advent Christian community, notes that "the distinctive beliefs and practices of the [SDA] denomination, while causing it to be viewed with suspicion by many traditional Christian believers, have seemingly given its faithful members a resoluteness of individual and group character that goes far to explain their successes." Dean Kelley sheds light on this dynamic when he notes that if people are going to join a church they want to join one that provides a genuine alternative to the larger culture.[16] On the other hand, Seventh-day Adventism (like Millerism) is close enough to orthodoxy in most central doctrines to get a hearing among other Christians.

Organizational Structure

A third element that led to the evangelistic success of Seventh-day Adventism was an organizational structure sufficient to carry on the mission and meet the challenges of its perceived message. At first glance it might seem that Millerism's success and that of Seventh-day Adventism might vary here. In a sense it does. But the variable appears to be time rather than organization as such. My essential point is that Millerism, given its brief existence, had sufficient organization through its conferences and periodicals to give direction to its mission for its few intense years. But such a nebulous organizational pattern would not have been sufficient to direct the movement's mission over an extended period of time.

It was the lack of sufficient organization that spelled the demise of the Spiritualizers and the lack of growth for the two Church of God Adventist denominations. Without sufficient organization they could not concentrate their resources for mission or maintain unity. Costly schism was the result.

It is at the point of sufficient organization that the Advent Christians and the Seventh-day Adventists also parted ways. The Seventh-day Adventist Church was the only one of the Adventist denominations to place significant authority at any ecclesiastical level above that of the local congregation. Hewitt, in bemoaning the plight of the Advent Christians, indicates that the lack of a "strong centralized organization" is one reason that "contraction threatens to overcome expansion" in their work. What centralized organization they did get, he argues, came too late and, worse yet, represented mere structure without significant power. As a result of their congregational structure, Hewitt points out that the Advent Christians were unable to mobilize for united action. With proper organization, he suggested in 1990, the Advent Christians might be "a growing and not a dying denomination."[17]

By way of contrast, two recent studies of Seventh-day Adventist organizational structure indicate that the denomination's structure was consciously designed with mission outreach in mind in both 1861-1863 and 1901-1903.[18] Of course, that does not mean that the denomination is without significant problems in its organizational structure. To the contrary, Seventh-day Adventistism, as we shall see below, is facing major organizational problems in the last decade of the twentieth century.

Prophetic Consciousness

The Fourth, and by far the most important, factor in the rapid spread of Millerism was its sense of prophetic mission and the sense of urgency generated by that prophetic understanding. Millerism was a mission-driven movement. One of the theses that I argue for in *Millennial Fever and the End of the World: A Study of Millerite Adventism* is that a sense of personal responsibility to warn the world of its soon-coming end literally *drove* William Miller, Joshua V. Himes, and their Millerite colleagues to dedicate everything they had to warn the world of coming judgment. Himes put it nicely in an editorial in the very first issue of the *Midnight Cry*. "Our Work," he wrote,

> is one of unutterable magnitude. It is a mission and an enterprise, unlike, in some respects, anything that has ever awakened the energies of men. . . . It is an *alarm*, and a cry, uttered by those who, from among all Protestant sects, as Watchmen standing upon the walls of the moral world, believe the WORLD's CRISIS IS COME—and who, under the influence of this faith, are united in proclaiming to the world, "Behold the Bridegroom cometh, go ye out to meet him!"[19]

That sense of urgency, it must be emphasized, was built upon an interpretation of the prophecies of Daniel and the Revelation. The Millerites believed with all their hearts that they had a message that people *must* hear. It was that belief and the total dedication that accompanied it that pushed the Millerites into tireless mission.

It was that same vision, based upon the same prophecies, that provided the mainspring of Seventh-day Adventist mission. From their beginning, the Sabbatarians never viewed themselves as merely another denomination. To the contrary, they understood their movement and message to be a fulfillment of prophecy. They saw themselves as a prophetic people.[20]

That understanding came from the conviction that they were the only genuine continuation of Millerism, particularly as that continuation related to Miller's interpretation of prophecy. From the early Sabbatarian perspective, the other Adventist groups had lost their way and eventually their mission because of their denial of Miller's principles of prophetic interpretation.

That denial took two different directions. One was a rejection of the literal interpretation of scriptural passages that seemed to be quite literal. Thus the belief that Christ had already come sapped the missiological strength of the Spiritualizers. After all, if Christ had already come, what was the reason for mission?

Meanwhile, it can be argued, the Albany Adventists rejected the stimulus to mission that had convicted and empowered Millerism when they rejected Miller's principles of prophetic interpretation in their denial of the great time prophecies of Daniel and the Revelation. Without that certainty of the flow of prophetic history, they lost their sense of conviction and urgency. They finally had to find meaning for existence in other doctrines, such as conditionalism or the nonresurrection of the wicked. That may have been good enough for a sort of denominational existence, but the Albany group had abandoned the mainspring that had aggressively propelled Millerite mission.

By way of contrast, the Sabbatarians founded their movement on that very mainspring. They not only maintained Miller's prophetic scheme of interpretation, but they extended it in such a way as to give meaning to both their disappointment and the remaining time before Christ's advent. Central to that extended interpretation were Christ's work of pre-advent judgment in the cleansing of the heavenly sanctuary and the progressive nature of the three angels' messages of Revelation 14.[21]

Those two prophetic extensions provided the Sabbatarians with the same sense of urgency that had inspired the Millerites in the 1840s. While the Sabbatarians saw Miller and Charles Fitch, respectively, as the initiators of the first and second angels' messages, they saw their own movement with its emphasis on the commandments of God as initiating the third. Thus, they believed, conflict over their unique Sabbath doctrine would be a focal point in the great struggle between good and evil immediately before the second coming.[22]

Prophetic Mission

That interpretation was reinforced by their view of the end-time struggle over the commandments of God pictured in Revelation 12:17 and the fuller exposition of that verse in Revelation 13 and 14. As a result, the Sabbatarians were convinced that not only were they the heir of Millerism, but their movement had been predicted by God to preach the three angels' messages to all the world immediately before Revelation 14's great end-time harvest.

That prophetic understanding did the same thing for Sabbatarian Adventists that it had done for Millerites. It eventually drove them to mission. By 1994 the conviction that their movement is a movement of prophecy had resulted in one of the most widespread mission outreach programs in the history of Christianity. By that year they had established work in 209 of the 236 nations then recognized by the United Nations.[23]

That kind of dedication did not come by accident; it was the direct result of prophetic conviction of their responsibility. Central to that prophetic conviction was the imperative to the first angel of Revelation 14:6 to preach "to every nation, and kindred, and tongue, and people" and the command of Revelation 10:11 that the disappointed ones "must prophesy again before many peoples, and nations, and tongues, and kings."

Clyde Hewitt, in seeking to explain the success of the Seventh-day Adventists as opposed to the attrition faced by his Advent Christians, touched upon an essential element when he noted that "Seventh-day Adventists are convinced that they have been divinely ordained to carry on the prophetic work started by William Miller. They are dedicated to the task."[24]

In contrast to that conviction, Hewitt's father wrote to F. D. Nichol in 1944 that the Advent Christians had given up Miller's interpretation of Daniel 8:14 and the 2300 days and had no unanimity on the meaning of the text. Another leading Advent Christian scholar interviewed in 1984 noted that his denomination no longer even had any agreed-upon interpretation on the millennium—the very heart of Miller's contribution.[25]

In short, when the Albany Adventists stepped off Miller's prophetic platform, they began a process of deterioration in their prior understanding of the end of the world. The seventh-day branch of the Adventist family, of course, have been quick to point out that Ellen White had predicted in December 1844 that those who rejected October 1844 as a fulfillment of prophecy would eventually be left in "perfect darkness" and would stumble in their advent experience.[26]

But it should be noted that merely holding the conviction that they have the "correct doctrine" is not a sufficient explanation for the spread of Sabbatarian Adventism. After all, the Seventh Day Baptists preached the seventh-day Sabbath with conviction, but their 5,200 members in the United States in 1990 is less than what they had in the 1840s. As one nineteenth-century Seventh Day Baptist preacher told Bates, the Baptists had been able "to convince people of the legality of the seventh-day Sabbath, but they could not get them to move as the Sabbath Adventists did."[27]

Likewise, many of the nonsabbatarian Adventist groups preached what they believed to be the truth of the premillennial return of Christ, but without the same results as Seventh-day Adventists. Hewitt notes that his "Advent Christian people have not been an evangelistic church" and have not made much of an impact on the world. The result, he points out, has been smallness. Not just smallness in numbers, but smallness "in dreams, in visions. Smallness breeds smallness." Hewitt also indicates that Advent Christian smallness cannot be attributed to unpopular doctrines. After all, he argues, the Seventh-day Adventist list of unpopular doctrines "includes all those of the Advent Christian faith and adds several more." In another connection, Hewitt roots Seventh-day Adventist success in their conviction that they have a prophetic mission in the tradition of William Miller.[28]

Hewitt's conclusions go a long way toward helping us understand the spread of Sabbatarian Adventism. Its mainspring seems to have been much more than merely the fact that the Sabbatarians believed they had the "truth" on the Sabbath and the "truth" of the second advent. *The driving force undergirding Seventh-day Adventism was the bedrock conviction that they were a prophetic people with a unique message concerning Christ's soon coming to a troubled world. That prophetic understanding of their mission, integrated with their doctrines within the framework of the three angels' messages, provided the Sabbatarians with the motive power to sacrifice in order to spread their message far and wide.* That same dynamic operated in Millerism. Unfortunately for Seventh-day Adventism, that very vision appears to be in jeopardy in the 1990s.

Vitality or Death: The Shape of Adventist Futures

The Adventist denominations growing out of Millerism are facing possible death. That is the inference of Richard C. Nickels, who concluded his 1973 history of the Church of God (Seventh Day) with a section entitled "A Dying Church?" The volume's ominous last words are from Christ's message to the Church at Sardis: "It was alive, yet dead!"[29]

Similarly, the final section of Hewitt's three-volume history of the

Advent Christians is "Should a Denomination Be Told It's Dying?" That section, published in 1990, contains a heart-felt analysis of the denomination's situation. The final moving words in Hewitt's trilogy are: "*I devoutly hope some are listening. Amen!*"[30]

Where is the millennial fervor that brought these denominations to birth? And what about the other post-Millerite denominations? Are they also in danger of losing their vision? In particular, what about the strongest of the Millerite siblings—the Sabbatarians?

At first sight it would appear that the rapidly growing Seventh-day Adventist Church has nothing to worry about. In mid 1994 the denomination had over 8 million members worldwide. Estimates for the year 2000 project a membership of 12 million.

The Problem of Aging

Yet all is not well. It is difficult for the older population sectors of the denomination to maintain their Adventist identity. After all, it is hard to keep people excited about the second coming for 150 years. The Sabbatarians face all the problems of an aging denomination that afflicted previous religious movements down through church history. Time after time the world has witnessed vibrant reformatory religious movements harden and lose their vitality with age.[31]

But beyond the issue of aging, some sectors of Seventh-day Adventism in the 1990s (particularly in such places as North America, Europe, and Australia) appear to be confronted with all the threats that eroded the other Adventist bodies. Thus in their search for meaning in the face of the seemingly ever-delayed end of the world, some believers are tempted to spiritualize the nature of Christ's advent. But to lose faith in an actual historical advent is to lose Adventism itself.

The Problem of Affluence

Alternately, affluence has made its impact on the beliefs of some members regarding the advent hope. The Protestant ethic of hard work and frugality has led many Seventh-day Adventists into cross-generational upward mobility. Several generations of such mobility can develop a membership that locates its kingdoms on this earth and has little felt need for coming kingdoms. It is easy for such members to be more at home with the larger culture than with their sectarian roots.[32] Many in such circumstances find it easy to downplay their denomination's distinctive doctrines. But such were the dynamics that spelled the end for Evangelical Adventism.

At the opposite extreme of the denominational spectrum are those who, in their reaction to their "less Adventist" Adventist neighbors, will be tempted to follow the lead of the Adventist extremists of the post-1844 period into the fringes of the Christian community. Some in this sector of the denomination are also prone to sectarian sensationalism.

The challenge facing the Seventh-day Adventist Church is to maintain a healthy middle-of-the-road balance as it seeks to uplift both the doctrines that have made it unique and those doctrines that it shares with other Christians. Both acculturation to the larger community and segregation into a sectarian ghetto sound the death knell for vibrant Seventh-day Adventism.

The Problem of Organization

A third tension faced by Seventh-day Adventism is in the realm of organization. On the one hand, denominational health is threatened by too much of a good thing. Nearly a century ago Seventh-day Adventism adopted a multitiered administrative structure that, in its trim state, was well fitted for mission expansion at the time. But decades of expansion and change have created a bureaucracy that is extremely expensive to maintain and appears to be becoming progressively dysfunctional in fostering the mission of the church in the most efficient manner. While the early 1990s have seen efforts at reform, the results have been minimal. Few in the denomination's power structure seem to be able to think through thoroughly the massive organizational changes necessitated by a century of internal and external change. Few seem to be able to catch the vision of possible new structural models for world mission in the twenty-first century.

At the other extreme are large segments of Seventh-day Adventists who are tired of paying the cost of the administrative machinery. These members see the future of the denomination in congregational terms. That route, of course, is the one followed by all branches of Millerite Adventism except the Sabbatarians. For them, congregationalism resulted in denominations that were weak in ability to maintain their own identity and unable to focus resources on extended mission efficiently.

Thus it appears that Seventh-day Adventism is faced, on the one hand, with the increasing weight of a superstructure that could eventually crush the movement itself. On the other hand, it is faced with the quite real threat of congregationalism. Success would seem to lie in coming to grips with the compromises and structural changes that need to be made if Seventh-day Adventism is to continue to be a viable international movement capable of operating efficiently toward accomplishing its perceived mission.

The Problem of Overinstitutionalism

Clearly related to Sabbatarian Adventism's organizational dilemma is its inclination toward overinstitutionalism. There is a tendency for its extensive educational, publishing, conference, and medical institutions to become ends in themselves rather than means for the end of taking the denomination's peculiar message "to every nation, and kindred, and tongue, and people." Thus there is the danger of the denomination gaining its self-image from its institutions rather than from its stated mission.[33]

It was at that very point that Joshua V. Himes, Miller's second-in-command, challenged the Seventh-day Adventists in 1895—a half century after the Disappointment. "You have," he wrote to Ellen White,

> many good and great things connected with health reform and the churches, with the increase of wealth, and colleges as well, and to me it looks like work in all these departments that may go on for a long time to come.... There is a great and earnest work being done to send the message of the third angel everywhere—but all classes of Adventists are prospering in worldly things, and heaping up riches, while they talk of the coming of Christ as an event very near at hand. It is a great thing to be consistent and true to the real Advent message.[34]

With those sentences, Himes put his finger on the tendency toward institutional and individual secularization in Seventh-day Adventism that was present even in his day. That tendency has not lessened in the past 100 years.

The Peril of Losing Our Vision

A final temptation faced by Seventh-day Adventism will be to give up its vision of itself as a people of prophecy, to forget its prophetic heritage. It is easy to see how that could come about, but for it to do so would be death to the dynamic that made Seventh-day Adventism what it is today. To deny its prophetic heritage is a certain way to kill its "millennial fever" and thereby destroy its missiological mainspring.

It is in line with that thought that we need to understand one of Ellen White's most oft-quoted statements. "In reviewing our past history, having traveled over every step of advance to our present standing," she penned, "I can say, Praise God! As I see what the Lord has wrought, I am filled with astonishment, and with confidence in Christ as leader. We have nothing to fear for the future, except as we shall forget the way the Lord has led us, and His teaching in our past history."[35]

---

1. See George R. Knight, *Millennial Fever and the End of the Word: A Study of Millerite Adventism* (Boise, Idaho: Pacific Press, 1993), 245-325.
2. David Tallmadge Arthur, "'Come Out of Babylon'": A Study of Millerite Separatism and Denominationalism, 1840-1865" (Ph.D. dissertation, University of Rochester, 1970), 306.
3. Daniel T. Taylor, "Our Statistical Report," *World's Crisis*, Jan. 11, 1860, 75.
4. Ibid., Jan. 25, 1860, 81; *Seventh-day Adventist Encyclopedia*, 1976 ed. (Hagerstown, Md.: Review and Herald, 1976), s.v. "SDA Church."
5. Taylor, "Our Statistical Report," *World's Crisis*, Feb. 15, 1860, 96; Feb. 8, 1860, 89.
6. H. K. Carroll, *The Religious Forces of the United States* (New York: Christian Literature Co., 1893), 1-15.
7. Kenneth Bedell and Alice M. Jones, eds., *Yearbook of American and Canadian Churches* (Nashville, Tenn.: Abingdon, 1992), 270-277.
8. Benson Y. Landis, ed., *Yearbook of American Churches* (New York: National Council of Churches of Christ, 1959), 253; Clyde E. Hewitt, *Midnight and Morning* (Charlotte, N.C.: Venture Books, 1983), 267.
9. George R. Knight, *Anticipating the Advent: A Brief History of Aventism* (Boise, Idaho: Pacific Press, 1993), 120, 122; Hewitt, *Midnight and Morning*, 275.
10. David L. Rowe, *Thunder and Trumpets: Millerites and Dissenting Religion in Upstate New York, 1800-1850* (Chico, Calif.: Scholars Press, 1985), 48, 70, 71, 93.
11. Michael Barkun, *Crucible of the Millennium: The Burned-over District of New York in the 1840s* (Syracuse, N.Y.: Syracuse University Press, 1986), 103, 111, 112, 117-119, 139, 143.
12. Howard B. Weeks, *Adventist Evangelism in the Twentieth Century* (Washington, D.C.: Review and Herald, 1969), 78-85; Timothy P. Weber, *Living in the Shadow of the Second Coming: American Premillennialism, 1875-1982* (Grand Rapids, Mich.: Zondervan, 1983), 127; Barkun, *Crucible of the Millennium*, 152.
13. Ruth Alden Doan, *The Miller Heresy, Millennialism, and American Culture* (Philadelphia: Temple University Press, 1987); Ruth Alden Doane, "Millerism and Evangelical Culture," in *The Disappointed: Millerism and Millenarianism in the Nineteenth Century*, ed. Ronald L. Numbers and Jonathan M. Butler (Bloomington, Ind.: Indiana University Press, 1987), 12, 13; Whitney R. Cross, *The Burned-over District: The Social and Intellectual History of Enthusiastic Religion in Western New York, 1800-1850* (Ithaca, N.Y.: Cornell University Press, 1950), 291; Ernest R. Sandeen, "Millennialism," in *The Rise of Adventism: Religion and Society in Mid-Nineteenth Century America*, ed. Edwin R. Gaustad (New York: Harper and Row, 1974), 112.
14. For more information on Starkweather, see Knight, *Millennial Fever*, 174-177; for more on Gorgas, see *Millennial Fever*, 211, 212; Francis D. Nichol, *The Midnight Cry* (Washington, D.C.: Review and Herald, 1944), 342, 343, 411, 412, 505-508.
15. Luther P. Gerlach and Virginia H. Hine, *People, Power, Change: Movements of Social Transformation* (Indianapolis, Ind.: Bobbs-Merrill, 1970), 183, 137.
16. Hewitt, *Midnight and Morning*, 277; Walter R. Martin, *The Truth About Seventh-day Adventism* (Grand Rapids, Mich.: Zondervan, 1960); Dean M. Kelley, *Why Conservative Churches Are Growing: A Study in Sociology of Religion* (New York: Harper and Row, 1972).
17. Clyde E. Hewitt, *Devotion and Development* (Charlotte, N.C.: Venture Books, 1990), 211, 341, 371.
18. Andrew G. Mustard, *James White and SDA Organization: Historical Development, 1844-1881* (Berrien Springs, Mich.: Andrews University Press, 1988); Barry David Oliver, *SDA Organiza-*

tional Structure: Past, Present, and Future (Berrien Springs, Mich.: Andrews University Press, 1989).

19. In *Midnight Cry*, Nov. 17, 1842, 2.

20. See Knight, *Millennial Fever*, 295-325; Knight, *Anticipating the Advent.*

21. P. Gerard Damsteegt, *Foundations of the Seventh-day Adventist Message and Mission* (Grand Rapids, Mich.: Eerdmans, 1977).

22. James White, "The Third Angel's Message," *Present Truth*, April 1850, 65-69; Joseph Bates, *The Seventh Day Sabbath, A Perpetual Sign*, 2d ed. (New Bedford, Mass.: Benjamin Lindsey, 1847); Joseph Bates, *A Vindication of the Seventh-day Sabbath and the Commandments of God* (New Bedford, Mass.: Benjamin Lindsey, 1848); Joseph Bates, *A Seal of the Living God* (New Bedford, Mass.: Benjamin Lindsey, 1848).

23. *131st Annual Statistical Report—1993* (Silver Spring, Md.: General Conference of Seventh-day Adventists, 1994), 40.

24. Hewitt, *Midnight and Morning*, 277.

25. C. H. Hewitt to F. D. Nichol, May 24, 1944, in Nichol, *Midnight Cry*, 455, 456; Interview of Moses C. Crouse by George R. Knight, Aurora College, Aurora, Ill., Oct. 18, 1984.

26. Ellen G. Harmon, "Letter from Sister Harmon," *Day-Star*, Jan. 24, 1846, 31, 32. See also Ellen G. White, *Early Writings* (Washington, D.C.: Review and Herald, 1945), 14, 15.

27. Bedell and Jones, eds., *Yearbook of American and Canadian Churches* (1992), 276; O. P. Hall, in Arthur Whitefield Spalding, *Origin and History of Seventh-day Adventists* (Washington, D.C.: Review and Herald, 1961), 1:257.

28. Hewitt, *Devotion and Development*, 334, 362, 357; Hewitt, *Midnight and Morning*, 277.

29. Richard C. Nickels, *A History of the Seventh Day Church of God*, (n.p., 1973), 364-366.

30. Hewitt, *Devotion and Development*, 267, 373.

31. See chapter 2 and Derek Tidball, *The Social Context of the New Testament: Sociological Analysis* (Grand Rapids, Mich.: Zondervan, 1984).

32. Malcolm Bull and Keith Lockhart, *Seeking a Sanctuary: Seventh-day Adventism and the American Dream* (San Francisco, Calif.: Harper and Row, 1989), 256-268.

33. See chapter 1 above.

34. J. V. Himes to E. G. White, Mar. 13, 1895; cf. Sept. 12, 1894.

35. Ellen G. White, *Life Sketches of Ellen G. White* (Mountain View, Calif.: Pacific Press, 1915), 196.

CHAPTER 10

Occupying Till He Comes:

The Tension Between the Present and the Future

"Surely I am coming soon" (Revelation 22:20). Those oft repeated words (cf. Rev. 3:11; 22:7, 12) are Jesus' last in the New Testament.

The early church, basing its confidence on Jesus' promises and on His completed work on the cross, expected to see its Lord come in the clouds of heaven in a relatively short time.[1] Yet Jesus has not come after nearly 2,000 years.

Unfortunately, time is a corrosive factor to hope. The passage of time left the early Christian church frustrated. And in the first four or five centuries its sense of premillennial immediacy was gradually replaced by a postmillennial outlook that viewed the kingdom of God as something that needed to be built up on this earth. Time and frustration eventually transformed both the church and its vision of the end of the world.

What did Jesus mean by quickly? I don't know, but apparently His definitions are not the same as the definitions of those of us whose life span is bounded by birth and death.

Of course, we should note that shortness of time was not the only chronological aspect of Jesus' teachings regarding the end of the world. The other was delay. Repeatedly in the eschatological (last day) parables of Matthew 24 and 25 Jesus refers to the fact that His coming would be "delayed" (RSV, see Matthew 24:48; 25:5) or that it would be a "long time" before it took place (NIV, see 24:48; 25:5, 19).

Jesus was apparently well aware of the tensions that His followers would face in the interim between His ascension and second coming. His main point in the Olivet discourse seems to be that His followers should live in the interim in a state of expectancy and faithfulness. Thus the several parables at the end of Matthew 24 and in chapter 25 direct waiting Christians not only to watchfulness but also to faithful service. In a related parable Jesus commanded His disciples: "Occupy till I come" (Luke 19:13, KJV).

That command is clear enough, but how is it to be implemented? What types of "occupations" are lawful or even permissible in the face of immediate hope but grinding delay? Those questions, among others, will always face those who take the New Testament's teachings on the second coming seriously. They certainly faced the early Adventists in the post-1844 period. They still face Adventists 150 years later.

Early Adventism and the Conflict Between Imminence and Occupying

The post-disappointment Adventists were thrown into an identity crisis second to none. Confusion ran rampant in Millerite ranks in the last two months of 1844 and in early 1845. It took time for the Millerites to sort out their emotions and beliefs.[2]

In the ensuing turmoil, two approaches to the problem of continuing time before the second advent came to the fore. The first approach stressed an immediate coming, while the second emphasized occupying during the interim, even though none expected the delay to be very long.

Those who held first and foremost to the immediacy of the advent continued to hold to the necessity of some sort of preaching and most of them became convinced that they needed to continue gainful employment in order to maintain themselves and their families. On the other hand, they stood over against institutional and contractual arrangements on the basis that such arrangements implied a delay in the advent and were thus indicators of a lack of faith in the nearness of the end.

Among those holding to the immediacy pole of their advent belief there arose the temptation to continue to set new dates for the second coming. Thus William Miller and Josiah Litch came to expect that Jesus would come before the end of the Jewish year 1844 (that is, by the spring of 1845). H. H. Gross, Joseph Marsh, and others set dates in 1846, and when that year passed Gross discovered reasons to expect Christ to return in 1847.[3]

The early Sabbatarian Adventists were not immune to the date-setting temptation. Foremost among their number in that regard was the influential Joseph Bates. In 1850 he sparked a time-setting excitement by interpreting "the seven spots of blood on the Golden Altar and before the Mercy Seat" as representing "the duration of the judicial proceedings on the living saints in the Most Holy." Since each spot stood for a year, Christ's heavenly ministration would last seven years and He would come in October 1851—seven years after the Disappointment.[4]

It was one of the other two founders of the Sabbatarian Adventist movement who opposed Bates. The July 21, 1851, *Review and Herald* carried an important letter from Ellen White on the topic. "Dear Brethren," she penned,

> the Lord has shown me that the message of the third angel must go, and be proclaimed to the scattered children of the Lord, and that it should not be hung on time; for time never will be a test again. I saw that some were getting a false excitement arising from preaching time; that the third angel's message was stronger than time can be. I saw that this message can stand on its own foundation, and that it needs not time to strengthen it, and that it will go in mighty power, and do its work, and will be cut short in righteousness.
>
> I saw that some were making every thing bend to the time of this next fall—that is, making their calculations in reference to that time. I saw that this was wrong, for this reason: Instead of going to God daily to know their PRESENT duty, they look ahead, and make their calculations as though they knew the work would end this fall, without inquiring their duty of God daily.[5]

This was not the first time that Ellen White had stood against time setting. From possibly as early as 1845, she had repeatedly warned her fellow believers that time was no longer a test and that every passing of a set date would weaken the faith of those who had put their hope in it. She also noted early on that "the time of trouble must come before the coming of Christ." Even her first vision hinted that the city might be a "great way off." Her reward for taking such a position on date setting was that some charged her "with being with the evil servant that said in his heart, 'My Lord delayeth His coming.' "[6]

Before moving away from the time issue, we need to take a look at several points Ellen White made in her 1851 statement against Bates's date setting for that autumn. First, she was against the "false excitement" generated by date setting. Second, by that time she had come to see the core of the Sabbatarian message as the message of the third angel of Revelation 14:9-12. She noted that "the third angel's message was stronger than time can be," apparently meaning that it provided a more solid base for their faith. And, third, she twice emphasized present duty over excitement.

Taken as a whole, Ellen White's 1851 anti-date-setting message is a powerful statement that she was among those advent believers who were focusing on occupying rather than immediacy. It is little wonder that the more exuberant Adventists were against her.

It should also be noted that her emphasis on the preaching of the third angel's message implied a process rather than a point of time. James White stood with her on both the anti-time-setting issue and on the Sabbatarian Adventist identity as being the people of the third angel with a mission to perform in gathering in God's people who would stand on the platform of "the commandments of God, and the faith of Jesus" (Revelation 14:12). They were beginning to get the idea that the Sabbatarian Adventists had a more substantial mission than had been perceived earlier.[7]

But James hadn't always stood against the setting of new dates. In September 1845 he firmly believed that Jesus would return in October 1845. At that point in his experience he held that an Adventist couple who had announced their marriage had "denied their faith" in the second advent. Marriage was "a wile of the Devil. The firm brethren in Maine who are waiting for Christ have no fellowship with such a move." That view, he later claimed, was held by "most of our brethren," since "such a step seemed to contemplate years of life in this world."[8]

Yet within a year James had married Ellen G. Harmon. The reason: "God had a work for both of us to do, and he saw that we could greatly assist each other in that work." After all, young Ellen needed a "legal protector" if she was to travel the country bearing her "important . . . message to the world."[9]

Between October 1845 and August 1846 a major ground shift had taken place in the thinking of James and Ellen White. They had perceptively moved away from the immediacy perspective of the date setters and had more fully grasped the occupy-till-He-comes horn of the Adventist dilemma. Their marriage is an impressive symbol of that ground shift. They had a work to do. As a result, they took the first step toward the institutionalization of Adventism. If the end was not to come as soon as they first expected, they had to take adequate steps to prepare themselves for service in the interim.

But they had not given up their advent faith. To the contrary, in the next few years they began to see that God had another message for His people to give before the great harvest of Revelation 14:14-20—that of the third angel of verses 9-12. Marriage for the Whites became a necessary means to the end of the furtherance of the preaching of the advent message. On the other hand, their marriage also pointed to their acceptance of the continuity of time.

As it turned out, marriage was only the first step in their putting Adventism on a more permanent basis so that the advent message might be preached with fullness to the ends of the earth. Repeatedly the Whites led out in creating stability in Adventist ranks so that the sounding of the third angel's message would be supported by an adequate institutional base. Yet at every step they had to combat those fixated on the immediacy pole of the advent hope.

Thus it was in the realm of education. As late as 1862 some believers wondered if it was "right and consistent for us who believe with all our hearts in the immediate coming of the Lord, to seek to give our children an education?"

James White answered that "the fact that Christ is very soon coming is no reason why the mind should not be improved. A well-disciplined and informed mind can best receive and cherish the sublime truths of the Second Advent." The same logic, he held, went for those who would preach the gospel. Thus the next decade saw James (with Ellen close beside him) as the leader in the establishment of Battle Creek College for the training of Adventist workers.[10]

It should be noted, however, that for the Whites education was not to be an end in itself. "Because time is short," Ellen penned in her first testimony on education (1872), "we should work with diligence and double energy."[11] In their occupying of the time the Whites continued to maintain a sense of the imminent eschaton.

The Whites also led out in the organization of the Seventh-day Adventist church structure. By and large, the Millerite movement had been anti-organizational. That stance had developed for several reasons. For one, time was short and formal organization was not needed since Jesus would soon come. Beyond that, many followed George Storrs in his claim that "no church can be organized by man's invention but what it becomes Babylon *the moment it is organized*."[12]

Some of the Sabbatarian leaders, including R. F. Cottrell, held onto Storrs' Babylon logic up into the early 1860s. In response to that position, Ellen White penned:

> I was shown that some have been fearing they should become Babylon if they organize; but the churches in Central New York have been perfect Babylon, confusion. And now unless the churches are so organized that they can carry out and enforce order, they have nothing to hope for in the future. They must scatter into fragments. Previous teachings have nourished the elements of disunion.... If ministers of God would unitedly take their position and maintain it with decision, there would be a uniting influence among the flock of God.... Then there would be power and strength in the ranks of Sabbathkeepers far exceeding anything we have yet witnessed.[13]

Of course, the reason the Whites had fought so hard throughout the 1850s for church organization is that an organized body could do more to spread the advent message. Their struggle for the institution of an adequate organization came to fruition between 1861 and 1863. As in their other institutional endeavors, organization was a means to an end, not an end in itself.[14]

The Whites led out not only in those institutional developments but also in such areas as the publishing and medical work. With each step they put the denomination on a firmer basis on this earth so that it could preach the nearness of the earth to come.

Both of the Whites saw the institutional upbuilding of Adventism as God's blessing. In fact, it is in the context of the "upbuilding of these institutions" that Ellen White penned her oft-quoted statement that "we have nothing to fear for the future, except as we shall forget the way the Lord has led . . . us in our past history."[15]

The Success Is Failure Dilemma

The Whites had faced the tension between the imminence of the advent and occupying till He comes by choosing to occupy in order that the Seventh-day Adventists could continue to preach the imminent coming. Unfortunately, there was (and is) a paradox inherent to the very dynamic that they were involved in.

There is a sense in which failure was built into the very success of the young denomination. That is, in order to preserve the message of the imminent coming, institutions based on continuity and semi-permanence had to be erected. And in the process subtle and not-so-subtle transformations took place. As Michael Pearson puts it, "the survival of 'the remnant' has been ensured by the mechanism of institutionalization, but that which has survived appears to some to bear little resemblance to the original."[16]

Joshua V. Himes, Miller's chief lieutenant in the 1840s, picked up on the dilemma faced by the Seventh-day Adventists during two trips for treatment at the Battle Creek Sanitarium a half century after the October Disappointment. He wrote to Ellen White in September 1894 that the Seventh-day Adventists had "done a great work since 1844—and still go on." But, he pointed out, "the way you 'build and plant' looks like a long delay, if present plans are carried out."[17]

Six months later, Himes (who had spent his last years as an Episcopalian minister) repeated the same sentiments in regard to Adventist institutions. At that time he went on to add that "all classes of Adventists are prospering in worldly things, and heaping up riches, while they talk of the coming of Christ as an event very near at hand." He went on to note that consistency and faithfulness "to the real Advent message" was important.[18]

Himes's last sentence implies that he believed that the Seventh-day Adventists had lost the essence of what they had started out to preach. While they still talked of the advent as near, they had come to live individually and corporately as if it were a long way off. As Edwin Gaustad has more recently put it, "While expecting a kingdom of God from the heavens, they [the Seventh-day Adventists] work diligently for one on the earth."[19]

Perhaps John Harvey Kellogg epitomized the Adventist dilemma at the turn of the century better than anyone. Kellogg stood head and shoulders above his fellow church leaders as a kingdom builder. Not only was he in the process of creating a worldwide system of sanitariums that would be controlled from Battle Creek, but he had begun his own medical school in 1895 (the American Medical Missionary College), and was the foremost Adventist proponent of a broad-based welfare work to the poor of Chicago and other cities. By the turn of the century there were more Adventists working for Kellogg's Medical Missionary and Benevolent Association than there were working for the combined endeavors of the General Conference.[20]

There is no doubt as to Kellogg's interest in mission and even to his initial interest in the mission of Adventism. After all, every student admitted to his medical school had to sign a pledge dedicating his or her life to medical missionary work. But Kellogg's endeavors brought him face to face with the Adventist dilemma between immediacy and occupying in a way that other Adventist leaders never had to deal with. The other branches of Adventist work were more insulated from the direct effect of secular culture and acceptance by that culture. Kellogg's endeavors, however, took place on the boundary between the larger culture and the church. As a result, acceptance of his contributions to society was a very real possibility. That potential acceptance proved to be a very real temptation to the doctor.

A case in point is the accreditation of his medical school by the Association of Medical Colleges. The school had been denied accreditation in 1897 because it was under the control of the Seventh-day Adventists and taught vegetarianism.

By early 1899, Kellogg, who had also been turned down in a cooperative venture for Chicago city missions by Jane Addams (a national leader in the social work movement) because of his Adventism, was ready for a new attempt to accredit his medical school. But he had learned the lesson of the first attempt well. A series of letters between Kellogg and the key man in the accreditation process indicate the extent to which the doctor was willing to go to gain acceptance. Not only did he claim that he did "not believe in such a thing as a sectarian school of any kind, either medical or theological," but he went on to feature his heterodoxy. "I am just as heterodox as you are," he penned. "I believe in the natural not the supernatural." He then indicated that to the best of his knowledge all of his colleagues believed as he did. He even went so far as to downplay his convictions on vegetarianism and diet, claiming that he had no more of a creed on those points than on religious issues.[21]

Such statements, made in private letters to non-Adventists, diametrically opposed much of what he had to say to church leaders. But such was the price of the politics of acceptance. The point to note is that in the hands of Kellogg, the mentality undergirding Adventist health and welfare work had gone through a radical transformation. Starting out as institutions for the furtherance of the message of the third angel, they had become institutions for the good of humanity. Institutional expansion and acceptance had become the goal rather than the furtherance of the Adventist message and mission. And in order to successfully work with outsiders, Kellogg had found it profitable to mute his Adventism.

Ellen White stood against Kellogg's bid for acceptance and his moves toward secularizing Adventism's medical missionary work. "The Lord," she penned in 1900, "has signified that the missionary, health-restorative gospel shall never be separated from the ministry of the word." And in connection with Kellogg's city welfare work she noted that it was a "good work," but claimed that it had "its place in connection with [rather than separate from] the proclamation of the third angel's message and the reception of Bible truth." Mrs. White also opposed the doctor's desire to develop the medical missionary cause disproportionately in relation to the other efforts of the denomination. "As the right arm is to the body," she cautioned, "so is the medical missionary work to the third angel's message. But the right arm is not to become the whole body." She was especially concerned that the Adventists perform their unique preaching ministry of waking up the world, since many of the tasks that burdened Kellogg "the world would do largely, but the world will not do the work which God has committed to His people."[22]

In short, Ellen White was calling Kellogg back to his original focus and the medical work back to the purpose for which it had been established in the first place. She was calling it back to its missiological purpose in relation to the denomination's preaching of the third angel's message. That call was a call back to the balance between imminence and occupying that had prompted the institutionalization of Adventism in the first place.

But the doctor had his own agenda by the turn of the century. Occupying had become the whole for him and imminence both a bother and an embarrassment. He would leave the denomination early in the new century so that he could operate his philanthropic work apart from the hindrances of Adventism.

The Tension Between Imminence and Occupying Lives On

The Whites, Bates, and Kellogg are long gone, but Adventism continues to exist in the seemingly unending tension between imminence and occupying till He comes. Adventists are still struggling with the tension between those aspects of the second advent; aspects its founders had to face 150 years ago and the early church some 1800 years before them.

A glance at the General Conference's 1993 statistical report indicates that the church is doing exuberantly well in occupying. As of December 31, 1993, it had 539 union and local conferences/missions, 39,920 congregations, 4,492 primary schools, 953 secondary schools, 85 colleges and universities, 35 food industries, 148 hospitals and sanitariums, 92 retirement homes and orphanages, 354 clinics and dispensaries, 7 media centers, and 56 publishing houses. These institutions employed some 136,539 workers.[23] The denomination's extensive international development and relief work (ADRA) was in addition to those figures.

Adventism has indeed become good at occupying. But the nagging question arises as to the purpose of the occupation. And that question raises the issue of Adventist identity.

Adventist Identity in Relation to Time and Change

Identity is a central issue to all Christian bodies. Understandings of identity and a church's role in the scheme of history provide purpose and direction. Needless to say, perceptions of identity are not static. They change with time. Those changes can be good or bad, depending upon the frame of reference.

Closely connected to identity is time. Time can have a corrosive effect on identity. That is especially true for groups expecting the soon-coming of Christ. The passage of time raises questions and presents problems and challenges that never had to be faced by a movement's founders.

The corrosive effects of time transformed the early church from a premillennial to a postmillennial mentality. And the effects of time are operating within Adventism today. With Adventism, of course, the results are yet to be seen. But after 150 years the questions of what Adventism is and what it should be about are of crucial importance, and they are being asked with increasing frequency.

In some ways questions of identity and purpose are not new to Adventism. In other places I have sought to demonstrate that a search for identity is the primary issue that has been at the center of Adventist theological development since 1844. That was certainly true in the wake of the confusion of the 1844 Disappointment and it seems to be just as true in 1994 as the various theological factions within the church put forth their views of genuine Adventism or of what Adventism should stand for.[24] The question of Adventist identity must not be downplayed. After all, the answer will provide future directions in the realm of theology, in the area of church and institutional structure, and in the role that Adventism will play in the world as it seeks to perform its ministry.

Intimately related to time in relation to identity is the issue of change. Change not only operates within the church, it is a major factor in the world in which the church exists and seeks to minister. Change is certain, and the way a church relates to change is absolutely crucial to its identity. A church can relate to change in healthy or unhealthy ways.

Change stimulated the rise of Seventh-day Adventism. Adventism's founders in the post-1844 period lived in a changed world, a world that forced them to redefine themselves, a world that forced them to rethink the nature of history and their place in it. Malcolm Bull and Keith Lockhart illustrate one aspect of that new challenge when they write that "a movement that first defined itself with reference to the future began to perceive itself also in terms of the past."[25]

Suddenly and unexpectedly the past took on new meanings for the Millerite Adventists in the post-1844 period. Either God had led them or they had been deluded. Relating to their past history had become an important aspect of their identity.

The past and God's leading in the past is a central feature in the Judeo-Christian tradition. Thus creation by divine fiat, the Fall, the Exodus, and the incarnation, virgin birth, death, resurrection, and ascension of Jesus have provided anchor points for Christian identity. Those Christian groups that have denied the historicity of those events have also spiritualized the Bible's teaching on the second advent. Such groups have transformed their identity from being primarily redemptive outposts to being essentially ethical and/or cultural societies. Many of the things they do and proclaim may be good and true but they have lost their distinctively Christian mission. They may carry the name of Christian but from the reference point of Scripture they have lost Christianity's content. And that loss of content has been accompanied by loss of mission.

In the Judeo-Christian tradition, losing one's way in the present begins when one's past is forgotten. The best example of Christian bodies that have lost their historic identity are those denominations associated with the Protestant liberalism that grew up between the American Civil War and the 1960s. In the wake of denying the supernatural in the Bible, the liberal denominations surrendered the historic anchor points of their faith. While these churches still exist, their health has degenerated along with the impulse to win souls to Christ as the only way to salvation. Their membership in the United States has shrunk by several millions of members in the last three decades.[26] A church that has lost its past jeopardizes its future and risks existing in a muddled present in terms of its cosmic mission.

Ways of Relating to Change

Seventh-day Adventism faces the same challenges to deal with change and history that have confronted other Christian bodies. There are only so many ways to face these issues. One is to live in the past as if the past can somehow be preserved intact in perpetuity as a golden age. Such an approach disregards the reality of change. In the long run its proponents have nothing to say to the present generation because they have lost contact with the realities that people are dealing with in the world at large. Such an approach finds mission only among those who desire to live in a past-oriented intellectual and/or social ghetto. Many Adventists continue to take this approach to change.

A second dysfunctional way of relating to change and history is to focus exclusively or almost exclusively on the future. Although having an opposite focus from those fixated on the past, this future-oriented focus has the same result. It loses contact with present needs and realities. Thus it also often leads to irrelevance.

A third way of relating to change and history is to focus almost exclusively on the present. The key word for those who take this approach is "relevance." And relevance is important. After all, irrelevance is a certain road to disaster. On the other hand, "mere" relevance is the road to nowhere. Relevance that has lost its metaphysical foundation, its biblical roots in the supernatural, is one more way of getting lost. Lasting Christian relevance must be rooted in the transcendent and in God's great acts in the history of His people. Relevance was the catchword of liberalism in the 1960s. But relevance without sufficient rootage ends up being irrelevant in the long run.

The Bible presents us with a fourth way of relating to change and history that is neither irrelevant nor merely relevant. This viewpoint is anchored in both God's leading in the past history of His people and in His bringing an end to earthly history at the second advent. But it does not neglect present circumstances and needs. Thus it sets forth a present orientation in the framework of the continuum of the past and the future. It presents a cosmic viewpoint that finds identity for the present in both history and prophecy. Thus its relevance, being rooted in the great continuum of history and change, is not transitory.

That position stands in contrast with Christian approaches to change that neglect the past, the present, or the future. From the biblical perspective, the line running from the historical past to the prophetic future provides perspective, direction, and identity for the present.

When Adventism or any other Christian body loses contact with either the historic past or the predicted future it will suffer disorientation in the present.

Modern Adventism and the Immediacy/Occupying Tension

In 1994 Adventism stands in a place analogous to that of its Millerite founders in late 1844 and early 1845 as it relates to the continuum of history and change and to the tension between immediacy and occupying. From one sector of the Adventist world we find those bound up with almost a time-setting frenzy as they seek to live in a constant state of excitement regarding the nearness of the end. Their faith is based upon world crisis rather than the promises of God. Even their behavior is motivated by the "feeling" of nearness.

This kind of advent faith tends to be an "up and down" experience. It has failed to learn the lessons of Matthew 24:36–25:46. A healthy Adventist faith must be based on more than immediacy and excitement. A deep faith and a life characterized by watchfulness and Christian service in the interim between Christ's ascension and second advent is what is called for.[27]

Sakae Kubo points in the right direction when he notes that "emphasizing the nearness of the real coming in an almost time-setting way" will prove to be counterproductive and disillusioning when the excitement passes. We must live with the certainty of God's promises as the basis for our faith rather than "the momentary feverish excitement of every passing crisis." The certainty of the second advent is more important than its timing.[28] To miss that point is to miss the lesson that the Whites and Bates had to face between 1844 and 1851. Such Adventists have forgotten an important part of their past history.

A second issue that both post-1844 and current Adventists have had to wrestle with in relation to history and immanence is the reality of a literal coming-in-the-clouds second advent. In the mid 1840s some frustrated Millerites spiritualized away the literalness of the advent and suggested that Christ comes individually into hearts and minds. It is all too easy for modern Adventists to follow a similar line of thinking by interpreting the promises of the advent metaphorically, holding that the second advent takes place for each person at death, and so on.

Taking such a course is equivalent to surrendering the advent hope that stimulated the rise of the Seventh-day Adventist Church. It not only moves away from the plain teachings of God's word, but it negates the prophetic promise of the future. That line of thought leads to the abdication of belief in Adventism itself. It dissolves Adventist identity.

At the opposite extreme from those living on the frantic edge of apocalyptic excitement are those who are tempted in their frustration at the delay of the second coming to turn away from apocalypticism altogether. That course of action was followed by many of the disappointed Adventists in the late 1840s and 1850s and it is a live option in the 1990s.

But to follow that direction is to surrender the very core of Adventist identity. Millerite Adventism arose in response to a study of the prophecies of Daniel 7-9 and Sabbatarian Adventism enriched that perspective by emphasizing Revelation 12-14. The Sabbatarians saw themselves as the personification of the remnant message of Revelation 12:17 and of the third angel of Revelation 14:9-12. That understanding provided an end-time cosmic perspective that drove them to the ends of the earth with their peculiar message. It was not merely their doctrines of the Sabbath or second coming that inspired the Sabbatarian Adventists to sacrifice their means and lives to preach their message around the world, but those doctrines in prophetic context. They saw themselves as a prophetic people.[29]

Take away that apocalyptic understanding and you have removed the living heart of Adventism. It does little good to keep the name if the defining content is changed and if a sense of God's providential leading is lost. That was the rock over which Protestant liberalism stumbled.

And yet that temptation is a very real one for Adventism as it nears the twenty-first century. It is all too easy to become frustrated with the delay of the eschaton and the bickering over the exact meaning of the details of the prophetic symbols and thus surrender the clarity and centrality of the larger apocalyptic picture and promise.

The temptation will increasingly be to turn away from the preaching of Adventism's apocalyptic message and toward "doing something useful" in the real world. After all, doesn't Matthew 25:31-46 plainly teach that social justice and mercy will be crucial elements among those who await the return of Jesus in the clouds of heaven?

That is true but it is not the entire New Testament picture of the waiting church. There are two apocalyptic foci in the New Testament. The first is the Synoptic Gospel focus that emphasizes faithful ministry during the waiting and watching time (Matthew 24, 25; Mark 13; Luke 21). The second is primarily found in the Revelation of John with its portrayal of God's last day preaching message and earth's final conflict between the forces of good and evil.

Biblical Adventism in both 1844 and 1994 and throughout its history has been challenged to integrate both New Testament apocalypses into its theology and mission. It is not a question of either/or but of both/and.

Unfortunately most church members, and even leaders, appear to be more comfortable with one half of the picture or the other than with the whole. Thus those who are "turned-off" by the immediacy wing of Adventism are tempted to either "play church" or adopt the Kelloggian vision.

Playing Church and the Kelloggian Vision

Playing church is a popular sport among both mainline Adventist members and leaders. In essence the game is based on counting and maintaining. It can be argued that the worst thing that ever happened to Adventism was its learning to count. Adventism counts institutions, members, converts, money, and everything else that can be digitized or quantified. Unfortunately, quantity and quality are not necessarily related. Nor, from the perspective of Scripture, is counting necessarily related to victory. But counting is an enjoyable pastime that provides a sense of useful employment and well being—even among those who realize that the numbers *may* have little to do with the church's original mission.

Among those who love to count things there is a danger of viewing Adventist identity in terms of the size, number, and variety of the denomination's institutions and the size of its membership rather than primarily in terms of mission. Playing church involves a great number of activities as tens of thousands continue to keep the machinery running quietly and, of course, expanding.

Unfortunately, the machinery too often becomes an end in itself rather than a means to the end. As a result, it is difficult to modernize or replace it with more efficient models. The tendency in such situations is to progressively gain identity from the wrong things.

Somewhat related to those who are to some degree turned off by Adventism's immediacy/apocalyptic wing and like to play church are those who have a tendency to opt for the Kelloggian vision of Adventism. These often see work for humanity in medical and welfare lines as the focal point of what Adventism is (or should be) about during the period of occupation.

Michael Pearson suggests that Adventism is facing a replication of the dynamics it experienced under Kellogg's philosophy some one hundred years ago. He points out that the finances of the massive Adventist

Health System dwarf the expenditures of the General Conference.[30] Beyond that, powerful forces operating in the marketplace have done much to secularize Adventism's extensive North American Health Care System. Institutional prosperity and growth appear to be primary in the system as it now exists, while any distinctively Adventist mission appears to be an *extremely* weak "second."

Pearson also notes that the same dynamic is potential for the relatively young Adventist Development and Relief Agency International (ADRA).[31] While in many cases ADRA is currently much more closely tied to the distinctive mission of Adventism than is the hospital system, age and continued growth could easily negate that relationship in an agency that has the potential to eventually overshadow the expenditures of even the hospital system. In the process, Adventism's primary focus could be *unintentionally* redirected as ADRA's influence strengthens within the denomination.

Now, lest I be misunderstood, I am in favor of the tremendous amount of good done by the hospital system, ADRA, church organization, and other Adventist institutions. My point is that Adventism faces the same sort of problems and temptations from its current "successes" that Kellogg faced earlier. It is easy to mute Adventism's apocalyptic message in small increments in order to achieve wider and wider acceptance or to receive additional funding. Yet the third angel's message as portrayed in the heart of Revelation is still the focal point of Adventist mission. But it is all too easy to either neglect that fact or to redefine the message in such a way that it loses its historical and scriptural integrity.

Pearson perceptively states that the "degeneration of the church into a self-servicing organization is just as great a threat to its mission as over-extension of itself in social-welfare activities."[32] The problem from both perspectives is one of purpose, mission, and identity as the time of occupying continues and as belief in immediacy and apocalyptic mission are to all intents and purposes shoved into an obscure rear compartment in many Adventist minds.

The Postmillennial Temptation

Waiting for the advent is a frustrating business. In frustration it is easy to disconnect from the premillennial advent hope, except in name, and to emphasize doing good and even preaching social justice as Adventism's *unique* prophetic mission. In the process, Adventism's apocalyptic dualism and prophetic understanding gradually fade out of the picture.

As noted earlier, doing good and working for reformed social structures in the name of Christ are excellent in themselves, but they need to be seen and appreciated within Adventism's premillennial perspective. That perspective is rooted in the continuum of time that runs from the past and extends into the future.

Divorced from that continuum, such good works and excellent perspectives could evolve into a form of postmillennialism in which Adventism's primary focus becomes improving this world rather than the second advent. With that postmillennial vision, held implicitly if not explicitly, Adventism will have come full circle from the polar extreme of immediacy to the polar extreme of occupying. Thus Adventism could evolve into the ultimate eschatological contradiction—a religious body that has immensely succeeded in institutionalizing for preaching the advent near, but a church that has lost the meaning of the very name that originally provided its identity.

Learning to successfully live within the tension between the present and the future is the unfinished task left to Adventism by the survivors of October 1844.

---

1. Oscar Cullman, *Christ and Time: The Primitive Christian Conception of Time and History*, rev. ed. (London: SCM Press, 1962), 86, 87.

2. George R. Knight, *Millennial Fever and the End of the World: A Study of Millerite Adventism* (Boise, Idaho: Pacific Press, 1993), 231-326.

3. Richard W. Schwarz, *Light Bearers to the Remnant* (Mountain View, Calif.: Pacific Press, 1979), 54.

4. Joseph Bates, *An Explanation of the Typical and Anti-typical Sanctuary, by the Scriptures* (New Bedford, Mass.: Benjamin Lindsey, 1850), 10, 11.

5. Ellen G. White, *Review and Herald Extra*, July 21, 1851, [4].

6. Ellen G. White, *Early Writings* (Washington, D.C.: Review and Herald, 1945), 14, 15, 22; cf. 75.

7. James White, "Our Present Work," *Review and Herald*, August 19, 1851, 12, 13; James White, "The Third Angel's Message," *Present Truth*, April 1850, 65-69; James White to Brother and Sister Hastings, Aug. 26, 1848; James White to Brother Bowles, Nov. 8, 1849.

8. James White, "Watchman, What of the Night?" *The Day-Star*, Sept. 20, 1845, 25, 26; James White, "Letter to Bro. Jacobs," *The Day-Star*, Oct. 11, 1845, 47; [James White and Ellen G. White], *Life Sketches: Ancestry, Early Life, Christian Experience and Extensive Labors, of Elder James White, and His Wife, Mrs. Ellen G. White* (Battle Creek, Mich.: Seventh-day Adventist Pub. Assn., 1888), 126.

9. [J. and E. G. White], *Life Sketches* (1888 ed.), 126, 238.

10. W. H. Ball and James White, "Questions and Answers," *Review and Herald*, Dec. 23, 1862, 29; Roy E. Graham, "James White: Initiator," in *Early Adventist Educators*, ed. George R. Knight (Berrien Springs, Mich.: Andrews University Press, 1983), 11-25.

11. Ellen G. White, *Testimonies for the Church* (Mountain View, Calif.: Pacific Press, 1948), 3:159.

12. George Storrs, "Come Out of Her My People," *Midnight Cry*, Feb. 15, 1844, 238.

13. R. F. Cottrell, "Making Us a Name," *Review and Herald*, March 22, 1860, 140, 141; Ellen G. White, "Communication From Sister White," *Review and Herald*, Aug. 27, 1861, 101, 102.

14. See Andrew G. Mustard, *James White and SDA Organization, 1844-1881* (Berrien Springs, Mich.: Andrews University Press, 1988); Barry David Oliver, *SDA Organizational Structure: Past,*

Present and Future (Berrien Springs, Mich.: Andrews University Press, 1989).

15. Ellen G. White, *Life Sketches of Ellen G. White* (Mountain View, Calif.: Pacific Press, 1915), 196.

16. Michael Pearson, *Millennial Dreams and Moral Dilemmas: Seventh-day Adventists and Contemporary Ethics* (Cambridge: Cambridge University Press, 1990), 26.

17. J. V. Himes to E. G. White, Sept. 12, 1894.

18. J. V. Himes to E. G. White, Mar. 13, 1895.

19. Edwin Scott Gaustad, *Historical Atlas of Religion in America* (New York: Harper & Row, 1962), 115.

20. Richard W. Schwarz, "Adventism's Social Gospel Advocate: John Harvey Kellogg," *Spectrum*, Spring 1969, 15-28; Richard William Schwarz, "John Harvey Kellogg: American Health Reformer," Ph.D. dissertation, University of Michigan, 1964, 347.

21. Schwarz, "Adventism's Social Gospel Advocate," 18; Dudley S. Reynolds to Robert Levy, Jan. 6, 1899; Dudley S. Reynolds to J. H. Kellogg, Jan. 17, 1899, Jan. 24, 1899; Memo from the Council of the Association of Medical Colleges, June 2, 1897; J. H. Kellogg to Dudley S. Reynolds, Jan. 19, 1899, Jan. 26, 1899.

22. E. G. White to Bro. and Sis. Irwin, Jan. 1, 1900; Ellen G. White, "The Work for This Time," unpublished manuscript, Jan. 25, 1899. See also Jonathan Butler, "Ellen G. White and the Chicago Mission," *Spectrum*, Winter 1970, 41-51; E. G. White, *Testimonies for the Church*, 8:185.

23. *131st Annual Statistical Report—1993* (Silver Spring, Md.: General Conference of Seventh-day Adventists, [1994]), 2, 3, 31.

24. George R. Knight, "Adventist Theology: 1844-1994," *Ministry*, August 1994, 10-13, 25.

25. Malcolm Bull and Keith Lockhart, *Seeking a Sanctuary: Seventh-day Adventism and the American Dream* (New York: Harper & Row, 1989), 34.

26. Richard H. Ostling, "The Church Search," *Time*, April 5, 1993, 44-49; Dean M. Kelley, *Why Conservative Churches Are Growing: A Study in Sociology of Religion* (New York: Harper & Row, 1972).

27. Jon Paulien, *What the Bible Says About the End-Time* (Hagerstown, Md.: Review and Herald, 1994), 85-93; George R. Knight, *Matthew: The Gospel of the Kingdom* (Boise, Idaho: Pacific Press, 1994), 232-251.

28. Sakae Kubo, *God Meets Man: A Theology of the Sabbath and Second Advent* (Nashville, Tenn.: Southern Pub. Assn., 1978), 103.

29. P. Gerard Damsteegt, *Foundations of the Seventh-day Adventist Message and Mission* (Grand Rapids, Mich.: Eerdmans, 1977); Knight, *Millennial Fever*, 327-342. This theme also undergirds the treatment of SDA history in George R. Knight, *Anticipating the Advent: A Brief History of Seventh-day Adventists* (Boise, Idaho: Pacific Press, 1993).

30. Pearson, *Millennial Dreams*, 28, 29.

31. Ibid.

32. Ibid., 31.

A Final Word to the Reader

You have reached the end of this book, but not the end of its topic. Hopefully the end of the book will be the beginning of relating more responsibly to the issues it raised. Each of us has a responsibility as we individually and corporately move from the past and present into the future.

Change is a fact of life. It was a fact that had to be faced by the disciples as they struggled to form the early Christian Church out of the Hebrew tradition and the legacy of Jesus the Saviour; it was a fact that had to be faced by the heirs of the early church as they moved into what we call the medieval period; it was a fact that had to be faced by Luther and Calvin as they sought to renew the church in the sixteenth century; it was a fact that the heirs of the Reformation had to face as they drifted into the deadening era of Protestant scholasticism in the seventeenth and eighteenth centuries; it was a fact that the earliest Sabbatarian Adventists had to face in the post-1844 period and in their reorganization in 1901-1903.

And change hasn't come to an end. It is a constant in our world. Change may not be a comfortable reality but it is nonetheless a reality. And church history demonstrates that that inescapable reality may be related to in healthy or unhealthy ways. Perhaps the most unhealthy way to relate to change is to ignore it. Such an approach is the "stuff" of guaranteed failure.

This book has argued that institutions, formal structures, and even traditions are necessary if a church's (including Adventism's) message and mission are to be preserved. Yet those very items become a threat to a church's original mission if they are not kept flexible enough to effectively meet change across time and space.

The key words in the above sentence are *original mission*. The word *original* brings to mind Adventism's biblical identity—the identity that provides it with direction and marching orders as it confronts the world with the message of the third angel and the soon-coming Jesus. Thus original has to do with both Adventism's biblical roots and its historical role as a change agent in a world that has largely neglected its Lord.

Adventism became successful because it was willing to face change responsibly while keeping in focus both history and its biblical imperative. When Adventism loses the ability to face change dynamically it will be ready for the museum of denominational existence; it will have evolved from the likeness of the new wine skin that allowed it to expand and meet the needs of people to the likeness of a crusty old wine skin that has lost the flexible dynamic that made it successful in the first place.

Yet change must not take place for the sake of change alone. The key criterion in responsible Christian change is biblical mission. Whatever is not truly and firmly biblical is not central to Adventism, even though it may be deeply rooted in the denomination's "tradition." Likewise, those denominational structures and institutions that do not represent the very best ways to maximize Adventism's mission need to be phased out or revamped to maximize mission. Denominational institutions, structures, traditions, and so forth are not *ends* in themselves, but *means* for sounding the message of faithfulness to the soon-coming crucified Christ.

May God grant us wisdom, courage, honesty, faith, hope, and love as we seek to follow our radical Lord across the ever-changing landscape of the kingdoms of this world toward the Kingdom that He will more fully establish when He comes again.

Index of Names and Topics

Index of Biblical References